D1283498

*Curiosities of
Literature*

Curiosities of Literature

JOHN SUTHERLAND

With illustrations by
Martin Rowson

BOOKS

Published by Random House Books 2008

4 6 8 10 9 7 5

Copyright © John Sutherland 2008
Illustrations © Martin Rowson 2008

John Sutherland has asserted his right under the Copyright,
Designs and Patents Act, 1988, to be identified as the author of this work

First published in Great Britain in 2008 by
Random House Books
Random House, 20 Vauxhall Bridge Road,
London SW1V 2SA

www.rbooks.co.uk

Addresses for companies within The Random House Group Limited can be found at:
www.randomhouse.co.uk/offices.htm

The Random House Group Limited Reg. No. 954009

A CIP catalogue record for this book
is available from the British Library

ISBN 9781905211975

The Random House Group Limited supports The Forest Stewardship
Council (FSC), the leading international forest certification organisation. All our
titles that are printed on Greenpeace approved FSC certified paper carry the FSC logo.
Our paper procurement policy can be found at www.rbooks.co.uk/environment

Mixed Sources
Product group from well-managed
forests and other controlled sources
www.fsc.org Cert no. TT-COC-2139
© 1996 Forest Stewardship Council

Typeset in Garamond MT by Palimpsest Book Production Limited,
Grangemouth, Stirlingshire

Printed in Great Britain by
Clays Ltd, St Ives plc

Contents

Contents

Contents

7 *Literary Crimewatch (and Gunplay)*

8 *Who? Who? Who?*

Contents

9 Name Games

10 Readers: Distinguished and Less Distinguished

11 Mammon and the Book Trade

Contents

12 Wheels

13 Morbid Curiosity

Curious Connections: a Terminal Quiz

Introduction

HAMLET: To what base uses we may return, Horatio! Why
    may not imagination trace the noble dust of Alexander
    till 'a find it stopping a bung-hole?
HORATIO: 'Twere to consider too curiously to consider so.
HAMLET: No, faith, not a jot.

This collection of *Literary Curiosities* is loosely inspired by Isaac
D'Israeli's *Curiosities of Literature*. Loose is the word. D'Israeli's was
the first such venture methodically to indulge the unmethodical
pleasures of the literary miscellany. Flim-flams, he elsewhere called
them. A perennial bestseller, his scholarly flimmery-flammery went
through seven editions between 1791 and 1823. The *Curiosities* is a
grab-bag of bibliophile and antiquarian anecdote and literary lore
– witty, charming, erudite, and above all 'curious'. D'Israeli serves
up a pudding which is all plums.

Modern academic life seems to me more and more like a
Japanese car factory – with scholarship that could as well be
produced by robots. I suspect even the plum duff we eat at
Christmas nowadays is factory produced, and its plums inserted
by steely robotic fingers clicking un-merrily on their assembly line.
The silver threepenny bits have long since gone, on health and
safety grounds.

D'Israeli's 'old curiosity shop' is a welcome antidote. In this
contemporary *Curiosities* I have followed D'Israeli's potpourri
unmethodicality. Entries have clumped together into sections,
by a kind of weak magnetism, but not so as to create any

systematic order – which would, I think, work against the spirit of the thing. I like to think of the sections as little stewpots – with many ingredients, but a dominant flavour.

Like D'Israeli, I occasionally wander outside the strict confines of literature – although I try to start or finish there. Some of the pieces may be considered too unserious for even unserious readers; some boring; some already stale; some codswallop. Most, I hope, will divert. Driving the enterprise is less the intention to instruct, or inform, than to communicate the random pleasures which may be found in reading literature, and reading about literature. Why else read?

I am grateful to Nigel Wilcockson for sanctioning this project (at Random House's expense), Victoria Hobbs for arranging things, and Messrs Google and Xerox for their help throughout. A few of the entries have been published, in different form, in the *Guardian*, the *New Statesman* and the *Sunday Telegraph*. 'Thrift' – as Hamlet says to Horatio, apropos of the funeral baked meats. On, then, to literary baked meats.

'Curiousity is the very basis of education and if you tell me that curiosity killed the cat, I say only the cat died nobly.'

Arnold Edinborough

I

Literary Baked Meats

'Erst fressen' – 'Grub first'
Bertolt Brecht

Omelette Littéraire

Many writers have their idiosyncratic gastronomic preferences. Jack London, for example, was devoted to duck, plucked but very lightly seared. 'Raw', others thought. His nickname among those close to him was 'Wolf'. One would probably not have wanted to be too close to Jack at lunch time, while wolfing his *canard Londres*.

Only one novelist, as far as I know, has given his name to a dish which has taken its place in classic cuisine. Arnold Bennett, the bestselling middlebrow novelist, about whom highbrow Virginia Woolf was frequently rude, dined – when not on his yacht or in the south of France – at the Savoy, off the Strand, in London. He could afford to; Bennett sold a lot more books than Mrs Woolf. Almost as much as fellow south-of-Francers E. Phillips Oppenheim and Somerset Maugham.

Bennett was a big man at the Savoy. The waiters were circulated with his photograph, so that they would recognise him, and treat him as the honoured guest he was. And, as the highest mark of that honour, the Savoy master chef, Jean Baptist Virlogeux, created a dish in the master novelist's name: omelette Arnold Bennett. It's a rather gooey thing in which a *baveuse* ('runny') mess of eggs is artfully mixed with haddock, cheese and herbs.

The dish is still proudly on the Savoy menu, along with such concoctions as M. Stroganoff's beef and M. Benedict's eggs. It is also on the menu of other top hotels and restaurants in London's West End, such as the Wolseley in Piccadilly, where the waiters jestingly call it Omelette Gordon Bennett, or Omelette Alan Bennett.

Curious Literary Grub

Those seeking colourful taste thrills in literature might start with J.K. Huysmans' *À rebours* (roughly translates into rough Anglo-Saxon as 'arse about face') in which the dandy hero, Des Esseintes, creates a dinner party comprising all black food, served by negresses, on black china. A change of tone could be introduced with the 'white soup' which is served up by Charles Bingley's servant in *Pride and Prejudice*. The whole thing to be finished with the chocolate-coated lemon-flavoured latrine disinfectant tablet, Patrick Bateman playfully serves up, as a postprandial sweetmeat, to his girlfriend, in *American Psycho* ('it tastes "minty"', she merely observes, innocently). The heroic literary eater must, however, go thyestean. Thyestes is the luck-less prince in ancient Greek mythology, unwittingly served up a pudding made of his own sons for supper. It has become a favourite theme in literature. Seneca wrote a revenge

Alas, although his dish remains in print among metropolitan bills of fare, Bennett's novels have fallen out of print – even his return compliment to the Savoy, *Imperial Palace* (in which Virlogeux figures as 'Rocco'). For those curious to taste omelette Arnold Bennett, and short of the fifty quid or so they'll charge you in its home base, the recipe for the dish can be found on the food recipes section of the BBC cookery website. As for *le roman* Arnold Bennett? Try eBay, or the nearest Oxfam bookstore.

play on the subject, much translated and imitated in the English Renaissance. Shakespeare introduces a thyestean feast into *Titus Andronicus*. So gothic are the horrors in that play, that it ranks as among the least blood-curdling the audience is made to endure. Swift, mockingly, argues in his 'Modest Proposal' that Ireland's perennial famine can be solved by Hibernian parents consuming their too-many offspring, 'stewed, roasted, baked, or boiled; and I make no doubt that it will equally serve in a fricassée or a ragout.' In modern literature, the hero of Evelyn Waugh's *Black Mischief* discovers, the night after a drunken revel with savages, that he has unknowingly feasted on his girlfriend, in what he took to be a peculiarly savoury stew. He handles the news without so much as a regretful belch. The *ne plus ultra* is in Thomas Harris's *Hannibal*, where the monster of the title induces a drugged victim to consume slices of his own brain, lightly sautéd in a wok: 'Hey, that tastes pretty good,' says the auto-thyestean.

Dr Johnson's Gulosity

'Gulosity' is not a word in current use even at the high tables of Oxford, where the best words are usually to be found. It has a fine Johnsonian ring to it – appropriately so, since Dr Johnson invented it. Gulosity is defined in the Great Dictionary as a noun indicating 'greediness, voracity, gluttony'.

These words, alas, attach adhesively to the word-maker himself. He had a lust for food which, if contemporary accounts are to be credited, offended those of delicate disposition who happened to be in the Great Cham's fallout area. This is Macaulay's descrip-tion (writing, it should be said, from historical accounts, fifty years after Johnson's death):

> The old philosopher is still among us in the brown coat with the metal buttons and the shirt which ought to be at the wash, blinking, puffing, rolling his head, drumming with his fingers, tearing his meat like a tiger, and swallowing his tea in oceans.

Boswell, on his first meeting with Johnson, was immediately impressed with the great man's appetite. 'Some people,' Johnson informed the (then) slim young Scot, 'have a foolish way of not minding, or pretending not to mind, what they eat. For my part, I mind my belly very studiously, and very carefully; for I look upon it, that he who does not mind his belly will hardly mind anything else.'

He was, Boswell reverently thought, in the presence of '*Jean Bull philosophe*'. At least, when talking. When actually guzzling, our philosophical John Bull was something else:

> When at table . . . his looks seemed riveted to his plate; nor would he, unless when in very high company, say one word, or even pay the least attention to what was said by others, till he had satisfied his appetite, which was so fierce, and indulged with such intense-ness, that while in the act of eating, the veins of his forehead swelled, and generally a strong perspiration was visible.

Plates, one must assume, were lucky to survive Samuel Johnson's table-time assault unbroken.

Otherwise an uncritical admirer, Boswell confessed to an un-Boswellian disgust at his idol's table manners. And total amaze-ment. Was not Johnson a 'philosopher' and a 'moralist'? Weren't these roles normally associated with moderation? Moreover, Boswell had heard the great man, 'upon other occasions, talk with great contempt of people who were anxious to gratify their palates; and the 206th number of his *Rambler* is a masterly essay against *gulosity*.'

If one turns to that piece (published in the *Rambler* on 7 March 1752) one is minded to concur with the faithful biographer. The essay is a meditation on one Gulosulus – a character invented for the occasion by Johnson. For thirty years, this fictional parasitic gourmand has managed to eat magnificently at the expense of others:

> Gulosulus entered the world without any eminent degree of merit; but was careful to frequent houses where persons of rank resorted. By being often seen, he became in time known; and . . . he was sometimes taken away to dinner . . . when he had been met at a few tables, he with less difficulty found the way to more, till at last he was regularly expected to appear wherever preparations are made for a feast . . . When he was thus by accident initiated in luxury, he felt in himself no inclination to retire from a life of so much pleasure.

By artful sycophancy, Gulosulus feeds on twenty dishes a day, every day, and dies rich. And very plump.

'Gulosity' is a fine neologism, and the character is an amusing moral invention. But it is clear that when the great lexicographer looked into his mirror he did not see Dr Samuel Gulosulus. He was the least parasitic of food gobblers. He filled the Johnson belly with his own tucker: or, if entertained, he entertained back with the currency of the best table talk in history. But he did like his grub.

KNORR AND A NICE JELLY

The first three-course fast-food meal in literature is introduced (with dripping contempt) by E.M. Forster, in chapter 6 of *Howards End* (1910). The square meal (all too literally) is served up by Len Bast, to his lady-love, Jacky:

> They began with a soup square, which Leonard had just dissolved in some hot water. It was followed by the tongue – a freckled cylinder of meat, with a little jelly at the top, and a great deal of yellow fat at the bottom – ending with another square dissolved in water (jelly: pineapple), which Leonard had prepared earlier in the day. Jacky ate contentedly enough ... And Leonard managed to convince his stomach that it was having a nourishing meal.

The novelist, one gathers, would not be so persuaded.

The soup is, one may assume, a 'Knorr Cube'. The brainchild of the German culinary inventor Carl Heinrich Knorr in the early nineteenth century it was originally, and rather unhappily, called 'soup sausage'. 'Bouillon cube', a term which came into use at the time Forster was writing, rolls more easily off the tongue and down the throat. Conceivably, of course, Leonard may prefer the rival brand Maggi (introduced, with great fanfare, in 1908). Oxo cubes did not come onto the market until 1910, the year of *Howards End*'s publication and are unlikely.

The canned tongue, or 'luncheon meat', with its layer of jelly at the top and yellow fat at the bottom is, in all likelihood, from a Fray Bentos tin, the Argentinian firm which, in the mid-nineteenth century discovered so profitable a sideline for the

8

cattle they were slaughtering for their hides that by the time Leonard and Jacky sat down to supper, processed meat was their principal product.

The jelly square, with which the feast is crowned, is, indubitably, one of Mr Rowntree's cubed 'table jellies', launched with huge success into the marketplace in 1901. All the products mentioned above are still to be found on your local supermarket shelves.

As, one is happy to say, is *Howards End* on the local bookshop shelves. Time is the ultimate test of quality, whether literary or gastronomic.

COME AND GET IT

Bulwer-Lytton's *The Coming Race* (1871) is a pioneer text of contemporary science fiction – although not, alas, as well known as it should be nowadays. Bulwer-Lytton's narrative pivots on the 'Hollow Earth' idea. Grotesque as it now seems, this was something seriously pondered by geologists of the time, particularly, in America.

The leading proponent of hollow-earthism, John Cleves Symmes, Jr, was keen that the US government should actually sponsor a voyage of exploration to the depths, via the 'North Pole hole' and plant the Stars and Stripes. A small (underground) step for man (or, more likely, underwater – since there is no ground under the Arctic permafrost).

Hollow Earth theory postulated the possibility of a habitable world, and perhaps even an alien civilisation, beneath our unconscious feet. Verne's *Journey to the Centre of the Earth* is a rather more famous exploitation of the idea, as is Edgar Rice Burroughs's long-running *Pellucidar* series. Modern geology (see, e.g., the 2003 movie *The Core*) confirms that any subterranean civilisation would need to be 99 per cent asbestos to survive the magma and 100 per cent stupid not to come up for air every now and then.

In Bulwer-Lytton's novel, a bumptious American engineer drops through a crack in the earth's crust to find himself in an alien civilisation – aeons more advanced than even Queen Victoria's. This subterra is ruled by giant, quasi reptilian flying females (poor Bulwer-Lytton had a very unhappy married life). These über-fems are possessed of a powerful quasi electrical 'fluid' called 'Vril'.

Bulwer-Lytton's novel was a hit in its day. Never averse to jumping on any passing bandwagon, commerce saw an opportunity and seized it. The French war against Prussia was currently raging across the channel and the French commander-in-chief, Napoleon III, wanted a nutritious convenience food for his troops in the front line.

What Napoleon had in mind was a precursor of MREs ('military meals ready to eat') as they are called today and consumed by frontline soldiers in the sands of Iraq and the hills of Afghanistan. What was it Napoleon's great namesake had said? 'An army marches on its belly.'

A Scottish manufacturer, John Lawson Johnston, made a successful bid, and duly came up with what was initially called 'Johnston's Fluid Beef'. A million servings were commissioned. This nutritious, delicious, 'beef tea' would, it was fondly expected, do for the French soldier what spinach does for Popeye. Alas, it didn't: France lost the war to the solid-sausage-eating Hun.

It would be nice to speculate that the dripping, and ineradicable, contempt which the French have to this day for British cooking originates in those million doses of 'Fluid Beef' which John Bull (and *'les rosbifs'*) inflicted on the luckless *poilu*.

Johnston's was a nifty invention, but a terrible brand name. 'Fluid Beef' did not do anything for the palate. The company duly came up with 'Bovril' – from the Latin 'bos' ('of the ox') and 'vril' (from the novel). Bulwer-Lytton got no acknowledgement on the distinctive jars and to this day the Unilever website does not mention the novelist by name in their official history of the product, noting only that:

> The name *Bovril* comes from an unusual word Johnston found in a book. 'Vril' was 'an electric fluid' and he combined it with the first two letters of the Latin word for beef 'Bos'.

Fortunately for Mr Johnston, the novelist, who was very litigious, died in 1873 and did not live to see the vulgar, un-Bulwer-Lyttonian Bovril jar arrive on the shelves of the British shops. He would have certainly been on the phone to whomever the top lawyer was in London at that time. Authors too march on their belly, as none knew better than the author of *The Coming Race*. 'A book, forsooth!' 'My book, sir!'

POSTSCRIPT: Although his novels have fallen out of print, Bulwer-Lytton still lives in popular culture as the creator of Knebworth, the Gothic pile in Hertfordshire, which is familiar as the location of numerous horror films. A lady who has slept at Knebworth assures me that 'he walks', and that the clammy Bulwer-Lytton hands still grope, furtively, from the other side.

BOVRIL: AND WORLD DOMINATION

It was not just the beloved little British pot (and the failed French grub) which Bulwer-Lytton's novel inspired. In Germany in the early 1930s, the 'Vril Society of the Luminous Lodge', was directly inspired by *The Coming Race*. The Lodge was, reportedly, a pioneer in establishing the mystical Aryan 'swastika' as the symbol of Nazism.

Allegedly (things get very paranoid, and not a little improbable, at this point), Hitler himself was a founder member of the Lodge. In power, in addition to sending teams of scientists to Tibet to determine the origins of the Aryan race (whose time had clearly 'come'), the Führer dispatched pot-holers (that word 'pot' again) into caves and mines – and even across the snowy wastes of the Antarctic – in search of the portal to Bulwer-Lytton's underground civilisation.

On the lunatic fringes of the web there is much speculation about whether those explorations might not have been successful, and that Vril (and the Lodge) are behind the UFOs which have speckled the post-war sky. The race, it would seem, may yet still be to come.

Bovril in Space

The first three-course meal eaten in space (we're talking science fiction here, of course; and French cuisine, of course) is in Jules Vernes' *Autour de la lune* (*All Around the Moon*). It is eerily bovrillian:

> In escaping from the Earth, our travellers felt that they had by no means escaped from the laws of humanity, and their stomachs now called on them lustily to fill the aching void. Ardan, as a Frenchman, claimed the post of chief cook, an important office, but his companions yielded it with alacrity. The gas furnished the requisite heat, and the provision chest supplied the materials for their first repast. They commenced with three plates of excellent soup, extracted from Liebig's precious tablets, prepared from the best beef that ever roamed over the Pampas.
>
> To this succeeded several tenderloin beefsteaks, which, though reduced to a small bulk by the hydraulic engines of the American Desiccating Company, were pronounced to be fully as tender, juicy and savoury as if they had just left the gridiron of a London Club House. Ardan even swore that they were 'bleeding,' and the others were too busy to contradict him.

Bon appetit, bon voyage, astronautes.

MILK OF KINDNESS;
GRAPES OF WRATH

In putting together the 'Curious Literary Grub' piece (see pp. 4–5), I toyed with including Steinbeck's 'Milk-Shake Joad Flavoured', but decided against it as, so to speak, tasteless. The following will, I hope, not offend.

John Steinbeck's *The Grapes of Wrath* ends with one of the more famous scenes in American literature. Sheltering from the pitiless storm, the remnants of the shattered Joad family find themselves in a barn, with a starving man. They have no food, and have had none for some time, but the daughter, Rose of Sharon (deserted by her rat of a husband) is lactating, having just lost her baby:

> For a minute Rose of Sharon sat still in the whispering barn. Then she hoisted her tired body up and drew the comfort about her. She moved slowly to the corner and stood looking down at the wasted face, into the wide, frightened eyes. Then slowly she lay down beside him. He shook his head slowly from side to side. Rose of Sharon loosened one side of the blanket and bared her breast. 'You got to,' she said. She squirmed closer and pulled his head close. 'There!' she said. 'There.' Her hand moved behind his head and supported it. Her fingers moved gently in his hair. She looked up and across the barn, and her lips came together and smiled mysteriously.

Most readers, in my experience, read that last moment symbolically: only the poor can give sustenance to the poor. Dives will never help Lazarus; another Lazarus, however, might. John Ford's 1940 movie rewrites and re-scripts the end of the narrative to make just that point about the poor helping the poor. As Ma and Pa Joad bounce around in their jalopy, she tells him:

> Rich fellas come up an' they die, an' their kids ain't no good an' they die out. But we keep a'comin'. We're the people that live. They can't wipe us out; they can't lick us. We'll go on for ever, Pa, 'cause we're the people.

It's false to Steinbeck's novel, but right for the time – that time being Roosevelt's populist New Deal, America-coming-out-of-the-slump 1940s.

John Ford's ending works. Audiences have always loved it. Does Steinbeck's ending work? More specifically, even if it works as literary device, is it physiologically plausible? One of my students at Caltech, the scientific institution at which I teach unscientific things, embarked, for the purpose of a somewhat cross-grained essay, on an investigation of the nutritive value of human milk and how long, precisely, one suckle would maintain a fully grown man on the verge of death from starvation. The result of the research was not reassuring.

The bottom nutritional line is, my student determined, as follows. A healthy lactating mother secretes about 500ml of milk per day. That amount might increase up to 700ml in the first year of lactation with good health, no physical stress, and the right nutrition.

The calorific value of breast milk is 70 per 100ml of milk. This quantity fully meets the requirements of the average newborn infant. The mother in *The Grapes of Wrath*, however, has been malnourished and is herself not far off starvation. She has been abandoned by her husband, and is in a state of acute post-natal depression.

Assuming she would exude a full 100ml (very doubtful) to the dying man, it would be (according to www.weightlossresources.co.uk) equivalent to four jelly beans. And if, assuming she could, Rose of Sharon suckled him for a whole day – using up her say 300–400ml of lactation – twelve jelly beans is neither here nor there to a full-grown starving man.

POSTSCRIPT: Was Steinbeck, one wonders, inspired by 'Idylle', the short story by Guy de Maupassant, in which two strangers find themselves alone in a train compartment (we are not, incidentally, talking Hitchcock here). One is a young man, the other a heavily lactating peasant girl who is in great discomfort. As an act of pure gallantry (the Frenchman prides himself on gallantry), the young man offers to relieve his travelling companion. The French version is voluptuous (it translates as something extremely icky):

> Il se mit à genoux devant elle; et elle se pencha vers lui, portant vers sa bouche, dans un geste de nourrice, le bout foncé de son sein. Dans le mouvement qu'elle fit en le prenant de ses deux mains pour le tendre vers cet homme, une goutte de lait apparut au sommet. Il la but vivement, saisissant comme un fruit cette lourde mamelle entre ses lèvres. Et il se mit à téter d'une façon goulue et régulière.

Makes you want to learn French, doesn't it?

To Finish With, a Lorna Doone Biscuit

A rather forlorn query on the 'ochef' website (dedicated to all things culinary) reads:

> I saw a recipe that called for Lorna Doone biscuits. Being an Australian, I have no idea what sort of biscuits Lorna Doone biscuits are? Could you please explain?

It is not, perhaps, only antipodeans who are baffled by a mass-market biscuit which seems to have an odd literary allusion tagging along behind it.

'Lorna Doone Shortbread' was launched on the American market in 1912 (the same year as Hellmann's Mayonnaise). It was inspired by the many film adaptations of R.D. Blackmore's 1869 romance which early Hollywood had churned out. It has proved one of the more durable foodstuff products and is still marketed, profitably, by the Nabisco combine. 'Lorna Doone' is jealously trade-marked – for the cookie, not the novel. The product has made no inroad into the British market: sweet as our national tooth is, even though British readers have always loved *Lorna Doone* – a novel that was among the select band of Victorian classics to be given a big-budget TV adaptation, in 1990, starring the dashingly villainous Sean Bean as Carver, and Clive Owen as good Jan Ridd.

Blackmore's novel is set in the (English) West Country, in the seventeenth century, at the period of the Monmouth rebellion. The hero, Jan, is 'when measured without clothes on, sixty inches round the breast' (Clive Owen had a bit of trouble with this) and boasts biceps the size of other men's thighs. Jan is not an afternoon tea-and-biccy kind of fellow. He's more likely to tear off the hind leg of a sheep and eat it raw.

Nor is Jan's native Exmoor a shortbready kind of place. Shortbread, of course, is conventionally regarded as a Scottish speciality – as much so as haggis, porridge or deep-fried Mars Bars. One associates it with tartan tin boxes.

Blackmore's name 'Doone' also has an incongruously strong Scottish feel to it – as in Brigadoon, or the famous lines in the ballad 'Annie Laurie' ('Lady Scott' version):

> And for bonnie Annie Laurie
> I'd lay me doon and dee.

It is, oddly, not the first time that *Lorna Doone* has benefited from being associated with things tartan. Blackmore was largely unknown when he published his novel. The work's subsequent runaway popularity is commonly attributed to the fact that the reading public of the time assumed it was connected, obscurely, to the engagement of Louise, Victoria's daughter, to John, Marquis of Lorne, heir to the Duke of Argyll. As Scottish as they come (aristocrats, that is).

Louise was the only daughter of Victoria to marry a British subject, rather than forming a union with some dynastically connected royal household in Europe. Romance, not politics, was the motive. It was the Diana event of the time and (in addition to putting the obscure apple-grower, Blackmore, into the top literary division) led to a rash of pubs called the 'Marquis of Lorne' and the 'Princess Louise' across the loyal face of England (but not Scotland, interestingly). Some of them are still serving good ale, but not, alas, Lorna Doone cookies. You must cross the Atlantic for those.

The Ultra-Literary Biscuit

Paterson Arran's 'Brontë' shortbread (so called for entirely inscrutable reasons) is reported to be the top-selling brand among MPs at Westminster's Portcullis House. Cheering news for the Scottish Nationalists (the maker Paterson Arran – Scottish bakers since 1895 – is as Caledonian as their product).

The biscuit that takes the literary biscuit, so to speak, is Proust's madeleine, the redolent taste of which inspires the long ruminations of *Remembrance of Things Past*.

In an article in *Slate* magazine in 2005, Edmund Levin reviews the many recipes 'reverse engineered' from Proust's sketchy hints and deduces, from close scrutiny of the crumbliness and dunkability described by the writer that 'Proust's madeleine did not, does not, and never could have existed.' To put it bluntly: Proust didn't know macaroons from madeleines, or from Lorna Doones come to that. But who dares be blunt about Proust?

2

The Body of Literature: Heads, Lungs, Hearts, and Bowels

'And your very flesh shall be a great poem.'
Walt Whitman

HEAD CHEESE

When Thackeray was a little boy, his favourite aunt was alarmed to discover that his uncle's hat exactly fitted William's five-year-old head. He was rushed to the doctors – water on the brain (hydrocephaly) was suspected. Aunt Ritchie was reassured to be told 'that the child indeed had a large head: but there was a great deal in it'.

Thackeray's head, as busts and portraits made during his life testify, does seem unusually capacious. His forehead looks as if his barber would need crampirons to do the necessary.

When he died prematurely, aged fifty-two, Thackeray's brain was extracted and confirmed to be extraordinarily heavy: 'weighing no less than 58.5 oz'. This clearly satisfied contemporary curiosity as to the Showman of *Vanity Fair*'s genius. Great Writer, Big Head. Talent corresponds with hat size.

But, in grisly point of literary-anatomical fact, Thackeray's brain was not outstandingly big. The Russian novelist Turgenev, for example, weighed in at a jumbo 70 oz. On the other hand, Walt Whitman could only claim a measly 44 oz. And, to the disgrace of French literature, Anatole France's cranium supplied only 36 oz of grey matter. Caviar quality, doubtless.

In point of fact, slapping whose-ever head cheese (as butchers romantically call it) on a scale, like so much calves' liver, probably tells us less about literary ability than Cynthia Plaster Caster's famed collection of penises and breasts that are attached to rock stars tells us about musical genius (according to Ms Plaster Caster, everyone asks the same question and the answer is Jimi Hendrix).

HEADY STUFF

Victorian novelists were as fascinated as were their favourite aunts by the stuff between their ears. Many (including the magnocranial Thackeray) had themselves 'read' by phrenologists (specialists, that is, in discovering personality in the contours of the skull). At her session, on 29 June 1851, Charlotte Brontë's bumps were solemnly examined by Dr J.P. Browne working on a subject he only knew as a 'gentlewoman'. The brain that gave the world *Jane Eyre* was, the doctor determined:

> *very* remarkable. The forehead is at once very large and well formed. It bears the stamp of deep thoughtfulness and comprehensive understanding. It is highly philosophical. It exhibits the presence of an intellect at once perspicacious and perspicuous.

Dr Browne hits the nail on the head, so to speak. Ms Brontë sounds like a 60-ouncer at least.

We may in the near future know something rather more solid about the brains of great women novelists than their distinctive cranial protuberances. In August 1999 it was announced that John Bayley had given the brain of his late wife, Iris Murdoch, to OPTIMA (the Oxford Project to Investigate Memory and Ageing). The team's principal interest is Alzheimer's disease. But, who knows, they may stumble across something significant about genius. Where is it bred? In the heart or in the head?

And, if OPTIMA doesn't give us the answer, other laboratories may. In 2005, newspapers reported that:

An art historian at the University of East Anglia has teamed up with a leading neuroscientist and created a new academic discipline: neuroarthistory. Prof. John Onians of UEA's School of World Art Studies wants to use the new brain scanning techniques such as fMRI to answer questions such as:

- What happens in the brain of the modern artist as he or she works?
- What happened in the brain of an artistic genius like Leonardo da Vinci?

'We are finally unlocking the door to this secret world,' Professor Onians said. And, if neuroarthistory, why not neuroliterarycriticism? Something will have to be done about the rather unwieldy name, however.

ASTHMA AND GENIUS

In her biography of Edith Wharton (2007) Hermione Lee notes – in the context of Wharton's chronic pulmonary ailments – that asthma often correlates, sometimes fatally, with high literary achievement.

The 'fact' that theirs is an ailment of the certifiably famous has always been a consolation to sufferers. It is affirmed by the 'asthmatrack' website which, among literary wheezers, lists: John Updike, Charles Dickens, Benjamin Disraeli, Dylan Thomas, Joseph Addison, Pliny the Elder and, of course, the author of *The Age of Innocence*.

To the speculative mind, plausible reasons suggest themselves for the correlation between literary talent and asthma. An over-sanitary upbringing is one. Writers tend to originate in middle- or upper-class environments. The mop, duster, and flash-wipe are never far away. Some parents of asthma sufferers I've spoken to are sceptical about the flashwipe arguement. Others believe there may be something in it; Wharton's case certainly supports it. Young Edith, for example, after an infantile attack of typhoid was never exposed to the bacterial risks of the school playground, but was educated in her luxurious New York home: an environment as germ-free, by the standards of the time, as a hospital Intensive Care Unit.

Sanitary homes are not always healthy homes, or so modern science suggests. Sebastian Johnson, a professor of respiratory medicine, writing in *The Times* (10 Feb 2007) observes:

> We know that those who have very low exposure to infections in childhood seem to be more likely to develop asthma. And it could be that because of this low exposure they never develop the immune responses they should.

This, the article continues, fits with the so-called 'hygiene hypoth-esis.' This theory suggests that allergies happen because we do not expose our immune system to germs early in life, as the Spartans would lay weakly-looking babes naked on the mountain overnight to ensure they had what it took to be Spartans. Little asthma, one suspects, in Sparta. And lots of little coffins.

Children, the doctors now tell us, should not be 'pompeyed', as Dickens's Mrs Jo puts it. Spare the germs and spoil the child. But the hygiene hypothesis would hardly work with Dickens himself, consigned as a child to labour in a blacking factor by the filthy Thames and resident, for most of his career, in a London where, as he graphically describes in the opening to *Bleak House*, the particles of soot were as large as snowflakes and the gutters running with animal and human excrement ('mud' as Dickens euphemistically calls it). He must surely have had a good inuring.

Dickens is, I believe, the first novelist to have introduced an identifiably diagnosed asthmatic into his fiction. In chapter 30 of *David Copperfield*, where the hero calls on the amiable Yarmouth shopkeeper, Mr Omer, he finds:

> the shutters up, but the shop door standing open. As I could obtain a perspective view of Mr Omer inside, smoking his pipe by the parlour door, I entered, and asked him how he was.
>
> 'Why, bless my life and soul!' said Mr Omer, 'how do you find yourself? Take a seat. – Smoke not disagreeable, I hope?'
>
> 'By no means,' said I. 'I like it – in somebody else's pipe.'
>
> 'What, not in your own, eh?' Mr Omer returned, laughing. 'All the better, sir. Bad habit for a young man. Take a seat. I smoke, myself, for the asthma.'
>
> Mr Omer had made room for me, and placed a chair. He now sat down again very much out of breath, gasping at his pipe as if it contained a supply of that necessary, without which he must perish.

Not much literary genius in Mr Omer's establishment, we deduce.

Dickens, rather more sensibly, took opium for his asthma. It may be that his own bronchial tubes were worrying him while writing *Copperfield*, this most autobiographical of his novels. Dora's dog, Jip, is also described as 'asthmatic'. It is a very stupid, but lovable, hound; like its mistress. She dies after childbirth. Jip, faithful to the end, dies with her. Whether of asthma is not indicated.

A Pack of Literary Hounds – faithful as Jip, but unasthmatic

Argos: the dog who wags his tail when his master, Ulysses, returns after twenty years away. Dogs live long in Ithaca and have memories like elephants.

Bull's-eye: Bill Sikes's bulldog; so loyal that it throws itself to its death, alongside its dying master. Neither is any loss to the world.

Rab: the first true canine hero, a highly sociable Edinburgh mastiff ('big as a little highland bull') in Dr John Brown's novel, *Rab and his Friends* (1855). Edinburgh also boasts the most faithful dog in history, 'Greyfriars Bobby', who for fourteen years refused to leave his dead master's graveside.

PROUST AND ASTHMA

More ingenious than the too-much-cleanliness hypothesis about asthma are those which draw on psychoanalytic explanation (a line with which Hermione Lee is sympathetic, in her account of Wharton). The root of the disease lies not in the bronches, but the psyche.

For advocates of this psychosomatic theory, the star asthmatic is Marcel Proust. An acute sufferer, after a life-threatening attack, aged nine, all outings 'in the air' were given up. Like Wharton, he was taught at home, by tutors, in a climate-controlled bubble.

Boots: the first canine narrator, in Rudyard Kipling's short story 'Thy Servant, a Dog'.

Flush: a Biography: Virginia Woolf's take on the world of Elizabeth Barrett Browning, as seen through the eyes of the poet's cocker spaniel.

Iris Murdoch liked introducing her friends' dogs into her fiction. As her biographer Peter Conradi, records: Tadg, in *The Unicorn*, was based on John and Patsy Grigg's golden labrador Crumpet; the papillon Zed in *The Philosopher's Pupil* 'was based on Diana Avebury's three-legged shrill-barking Zelda'; Anax in *The Green Knight* was based on Conradi's own blue merle collie, Cloudy. If there was a Booker Prize (let's call it a 'Barker Prize') for naming canines Murdoch (herself dogless) would win hands down.

In an article, 'Asthma and the Fear of Death', in *Psychoanalytic Quarterly* (1960) Karem J. Monsour digs deep into the aetiology of Proust's condition:

> Asthma is said to be precipitated by separation or threat of separation from the mother. French, Alexander, et al. have formulated the concept that in asthmatics 'the nuclear psycho-dynamic factor is a conflict centring in an excessive unresolved dependence upon the mother'.

Mr Omer's pipe, and the modern ventolin inhaler are clearly poor substitutes for the maternal nipple.

In a Q&A session, after a lecture at the National Portrait Gallery in 2001, the writer Edmund White (biographer of Proust and a brilliant autobiographer of himself) was asked 'whether Proust's asthma was code for his sexuality'. White was sceptical: 'Proust really was asthmatic', he asserted, adding 'But it did turn him into a recluse and an observer.'

The author of *À la recherche du temps perdu* should, perhaps, have been even more reclusive than he actually was. Himself a prudent smoker of 'Espic' anti-asthmatic cigarettes, legend has it that the pneumonia that killed Proust was precipitated by an asthmatic attack brought on by the young Samuel Beckett's cigar-smoking.

So much for Mr Omer's thesis ('I smoke, myself, for the asthma'). Smoking Kills, as the packets threaten us. Guns, however, are quicker (see p. 141), as is liquor (see p. 250).

JAMES'S IRRITABLY (FRIGID) BOWEL SYNDROME

Reviewing the newly published *Complete Letters of Henry James, Volumes 1 and 2, 1855–1872*, in July 2007, Peter Kemp observed that 'Literature owes an enormous debt to Henry James's bowels.' As the correspondence revealed, the young Henry suffered from chronic constipation. To alleviate it his parents dispatched him on a grand tour of Europe (doubtless hoping the foreign food would loosen his entrails). As Kemp notes:

> Glum reports on the failure of water cures, laxative diets and vigorous hiking to dislodge his 'hideous repletion' went back across the Atlantic

to his brother William (a fellow-sufferer who speculates – 'Electricity sometimes has a wonderful effect' – on the possible benefits of applying 'a strong galvanic current' to the seat of the problem).

'Rippling through these letters,' Kemp detects, 'are the first imaginative stirrings of one of the greatest fiction and travel writers in the language.' Costiveness inspired the famously contorted style – sentences which labour, often interminably, to deliver their meaning.

If true, Henry James's IBS takes its place with other happy (for literature) afflictions: the polio that lamed Walter Scott, and prevented him from being the soldier that he always wanted to be; or the short-sightedness that made it impossible for Tom Clancy to pursue a military career, obliging him to write about it instead; or the TB, that gave Alan Sillitoe an invalid discharge from the RAF, a convalescent couple of years, and a sufficient disability pension wherewith to write *Saturday Night and Sunday Morning*. Without that happy (for literature) bacillus, the Arctic Monkeys would not have had their allusive, career-making album, *Whatever People Say I Am, That's What I'm Not* and Gordon Brown, who claimed to like their music above all others, would have had to pretend to like another pop group in order to certify his street credibility with the younger British electorate. Curious.

There is no need, however, to be over-grateful to the tubercular bacillus. It robbed us not merely of the conclusion to Keats's *Hyperion*, but of any successor to *Nineteen Eighty-Four*. George Orwell died when forty-seven years old (if that's the right word). Among the most poignant lines in literature is that in a letter to David Astor, in February 1948 that the doctors have told him about something 'called streptomycin'. This was a first-generation antibiotic that would, soon after, make TB as much a thing of the past as leprosy.

The rich and well-disposed Astor procured some of the new drug from America for his friend, but it was too late and disastrously mis-prescribed. Had the disease given him another couple of years, while the antibiotic cure was refined, Orwell might well have lived to see the year about which he was so gloomy – 1984, that is.

As Mrs Thatcher laid into those miners, about whom Orwell had sentimentalised in *The Road to Wigan Pier*, in 1984 itself Orwell might well have been inspired to even greater gloom than he experienced in 1948. To paraphrase O'Brien as he tortures Winston Smith: 'The Party seeks power entirely for its own sake ... If you want a picture of the future, imagine a Thatcherite handbag swinging against a human face – for ever.'

IRRITABLE BOWELS (II)

A vivid last poem – also, legend has it, his famous last words – is recorded as issuing from the tremulous lips of the Scottish Chaucerian, Robert Henryson (author of *The Testament of Cresseid*). Henryson died, probably around 1505 (no one is sure), of dysentery – or 'flux'. An eye-witness account of his last hours was put on paper by his friend, Sir Francis Kinaston.

Sixteenth-century medicine could do nothing for the venerable Dunfermline 'makar' – whom an off-the-shelf course of Imodium would doubtless have saved. None the less, they did what they could. In extremis, a white witch was called in. After due inspection, the old crone quaveringly told her patient:

> There is a whikey tree in the lower end of your orchard, if you go and walk but thrice about it, and thrice repeat these words 'whikey tree, whikey tree, take away this fluxe from me', you shall be presently cured.

Too feeble to move, but not too feeble to explode with terminal indignation against bad verse, Henryson, with his last reserves of bodily strength, pointed to the table in his room and enquired, sarcastically, whether it might not serve as well 'if I repeated thrice these words: "Oken burd oken burd Garre me shit an hard turde"'.

He died shortly afterwards, 'within half a quarter of an hour', as Kinaston pedantically records. He did not, one suspects, go gentle in the night; but still raging against the foolishness of witches.

Whether the whikey tree might have helped bring on hard turds, posterity will never know and medical science has not yet investigated. 'I hae me doots,' as the Scots say.

Ill Wind

On 5 August 2007, following the recently introduced total ban on smoking in pubs, the *Sunday Times* reported that, far from making the serious drinker's atmosphere more salubrious, the opposite had happened. Oliver Devine, senior marketing manager of the Sizzling Pub Company (wonderful name) was quoted as saying:

> Appetising food smells have increased but others are less attractive, such as stale food and beer, damp, sweat and body odour, drains and – how do you put this nicely? – flatulence.

Putting it nicely is, if one takes a long historical perspective, a recent anxiety. The Emperor Claudius gave a medal to anyone who broke wind in his presence and tried to get some 'let it rip' reforms through the Senate. Robert Graves has some fun with it in his Roman novels, although I don't recall the detail featuring in the popular TV versions.

The fart is found in the very fundament of the father of English verse, Chaucer. An eructation, fit to split the sky, climaxes 'The Miller's Tale', when Absolon, a lusty young lad, knocks on the window of his beloved Alisoun, the cuckolded carpenter's wife, beseeching a night-time kiss. The wily Nicholas, however, has got into her sheets before him and juts his 'ers' out of the window and, 'anon':

> . . . leet fle a fart,
> As greet as it had been a thonder-dent

The luckless Absolon is almost 'blinded' with the unexpected gust. Once recovered, his revenge is prompt, fiery, buttock-directed, and hilarious.

Elizabethan and Jacobean comedy is similarly redolent with fart jokes and allusion. The second line of Ben Jonson's *The Alchemist* has rogue Subtle snarling at his fellow-rogue Face, 'I fart at thee'. In some modern productions, he does just that. Later in the play, the preposterous Sir Epicure Mammon, fantasising what he will do with his wealth after Face and Subtle have given him the philosopher's stone, prophesies:

> . . . My flatterers
> Shall be the pure and gravest of divines,
> That I can get for money. My mere fools,
> Eloquent burgesses, and then my poets
> The same that writ so subtly of the fart,
> Whom I will entertain still for that subject . . .

There is owlish scholarly dispute as to who the subtle poet might be. A popular candidate is John Suckling, presumed author of 'Down Came Grave Ancient Sir John Crooke', otherwise, and more descriptively known by the title: 'On a Fart in the Parliament-House'.

Impropriety did not come into it. Even the most divine were unembarrassed (although they could be highly amused) by references to this particular bodily function.

Martin Luther, for example, is supposed to have asked one of his companions at table '*Warum rülpset und furzet ihr nicht, hat es euch denn nicht geschmecket?*' ('Why don't you belch and fart, did you not enjoy the meal?'). John Osborne elaborates this broadness of talk in his 1961 play, *Luther*, whose hero describes himself as 'a ripe stool in the world's straining anus'. One can't be sure the German divine would have gone quite that far after dinner. A fart and a belch would have sufficed.

One of Walter Scott's favourite after-dinner stories was of Queen Elizabeth, getting into a barge on the Thames and, as she stepped across, breaking wind. The bargeman promptly apologised on her behalf. He was knighted by a grateful monarch on the spot: Sir Bargeman of the Gracious Wind, perhaps. The story outdoes Sir Walter Raleigh and the velvet cloak, and is surely just as apocryphal. Scott, of course, would never have thought of intruding the impropriety into his Elizabethan novel, *Kenilworth* The bargeman story was for the smoking room.

King James, Elizabeth's successor, in his counterblast against tobacco, hints broadly that smoking means voiding sooty wind: filthy fumes fore and aft. 'Smoking Smells', as might have been written, by royal (dis)command, on the Jacobean fag packet.

ILL WIND (11)

In the civilising process, pioneered by Addison and Steele in the eighteenth century, this broad freedom of reference to wind ('gas' as the Americans call it) is sanitised out of English literature for a century or more. Civilisation, as Freud notes, is measured anatomically by the distance the human species raises its nose away from the brown towards the toffee. Not one character in Victorian fiction, as I recall, breaks wind. Even in pornography of the period, it is rare. Chaucer was strenuously bowdlerised, particularly for the classroom.

The pressure of universal decency on the topic was occasionally resented and resisted. Never more wittily than by Mark Twain, in his Rabelaisian fantasia, *1601*. The squib was composed around 1876, the same period that he was writing *Tom Sawyer*, and there is a congenial juvenile naughtiness about the piece. This, one is tempted to speculate, is the portion of the novel Twain could write, but not publish. At least, not under his own name, or through the normal channels.

Subtitled 'Conversation, as it was by the Social Fireside, in the Time of the Tudors' the eight-page, pseudo 'authentic' pamphlet was published, anonymously, in 1880. *1601* takes the form of a conversation in Queen Elizabeth's closet (her private drawing room) in the year of the title. Present in the company are Ben Jonson, Sir Walter Raleigh, and 'ye famous Shaxpur'. The conversation kicks off when:

> In ye heat of ye talk it befel yt one did breake wind, yielding an exceding mightie and distresfull stink, whereat all did laugh full sore.

Laughing with the rest of them, Elizabeth asks who was responsible for this 'thundergust'? Jonson pleads innocent, noting, however, that ''Twas not a novice did it.' Shakespeare also declares himself not guilty, with a volley of high-flown verse. Finally Sir Walter Raleigh confesses to the deed. But, he boasts, it was 'nothing' compared to what he normally manages from his 'nether throat'. The claim is substantiated:

> Then delivered he himself of such a godless and rock-shivering blast that all were fain to stop their ears, and following it did come so dense and foul a stink that that which went before did seem a poor and trifling thing beside it.

There follows a philosophical conversation on the subject, and sundry other improper things.

The bawdy freedoms Twain yearned for were a long time coming. There is not a single smell in all Hemingway, Norman Mailer once complained (on the Dick Cavett show, as I recall: I haven't personally sniffed through the Hemingway oeuvre).

Joyce, as with so much else in twentieth-century fiction blazed the trail in the opening sections of *Ulysses*, with the description of Leopold Bloom, 'asquat the cuckstool . . . seated calm above his own rising smell'. And after the liberating *Lady Chatterley* judgements the other four-letter f-word regained its traditional Chaucerian liberties.

In William Styron's *The Confessions of Nat Turner* (1967), for example, the imprisoned black revolutionary hero is described in prison being interviewed by his oafish white lawyer Gray (meaningful name). As Turner works out how best to get his case to posterity, Gray's posteriors shift meaningfully:

I saw Gray stir uncomfortably then raise one haunch up off a fart, trying to slide it out gracefully, but it emerged in multiple soft reports like the popping of a firecracker. Suddenly he seemed flustered, discomfited, and this amused me. Why should he feel embarrassed before a nigger preacher, whose death warrant he was reading?

Such passages in fiction become frequent, unobtrusive, and stylistically unembarrassed over the last half of the twentieth century. Many novelists, nowadays, could display a Claudius medal among their other decorations.

The Virgin Queen and Eructation

John Aubrey (1626–97) recounts the following in his *Brief Lives* about one of Queen Elizabeth's close courtiers (it may, one suspects, have inspired Twain):

> This Earle of Oxford, making of his low obeisance to Queen Elizabeth, happened to let a Fart, at which he was so abashed and ashamed that he went to Travell, 7 yeares. On his returne the Queen welcomed him home, and sayd, My Lord, I had forgott the Fart.

Thanks to Aubrey, it will never now be forgott.

HARDY'S HEART

Long before he died in 1928, Thomas Hardy had made it crystal clear (in his will, notably) that he wanted to be buried in Wessex, where he had been born and whose laureate he was, alongside his first wife, the great love of his life. The vicar at the church in question (even though Hardy – as poems such as 'The Impercipient' make clear – was at best agnostic) strongly prevailed on Hardy's second wife to acquiesce in the famous author's wishes.

The nation, however, viewed Thomas Hardy as a British, not a regional, treasure. They wanted him. Stanley Baldwin's government put its muscle behind the move to have the greatest writer of the time interred in Westminster Abbey (Baldwin was a great lover of rural fiction – particularly the dark gothic tales of Mary Webb, immortally spoofed by Stella Gibbons' *Cold Comfort Farm*).

An unseemly tug of war developed over the corpse. It was finally settled, Solomon fashion, with the surgeon's scalpel. Hardy's heart was extracted, to be buried at Stinsford. It was given, for safe keeping, to his widow. The remainder of his carcass (including the wonderful brain, which would have relished this posthumous comedy) was cremated at Woking, and later ceremonially entombed, alongside the great poets, in Westminster Abbey (he was cremated for logistical reasons – there wasn't room, what with the crowd of great poets, for a whole new body in the corner).

The compromise was clearly inspired by the similar arrangements which had been made for David Livingstone. Scotland's greatest missionary had died in 1873 in East Africa. His heart was buried in a biscuit tin under a mvula tree near where he died. His body, preserved in salt, was carried over a thousand miles by native bearers to be returned to Britain for burial in Westminster Abbey. It was marked with a day of national mourning.

The ranks of heartless worthies under the honorific flags of the Abbey are a highly select band. Hardy and Livingstone would seem to be all of them. Byron's heart was interred at Missolonghi, where he gave his life in the fight for Greek independence. But his body (too carnal by far) was not thought fit for sacred ground, and was refused entry to their soil by Westminster's moral guardians. It was laid in the family vault (an apologetic memorial plaque was put up in the Abbey in 1969 – even the Anglican Church loosened up in the swinging sixties).

So too with Byron's partner in the notorious 'League of Incest', Shelley. His heart and body were separated: the cremated ashes being buried in the Protestant Cemetery in Rome while the heart (plucked from the flames by his friend, Edward Trelawney) was brought back to be buried in Dorset (not far, as it happens, from Hardy's organ). Shelley, like Byron, was deemed unfit to lie alongside the virtuous in Poets' Corner.

The removal of Hardy's heart from his scarcely cold body provoked a national frisson of horror. It was widely regarded as sacrilegious and barbarous and more appropriate to a Mayan sacrificial orgy than England in 1928. Hardy's were the last famous literary remains to be so divided up for burial.

As the Hardy Society records:

reaction to the somewhat bizarre events attendant upon Hardy's death had prompted a good deal of sardonic comment, especially in the local public houses. Of almost instant creation was the still surviving joke in which God, on the Day of Judgement, demands (in his best Dorset accent), 'Yer be 'is 'eart, but where be rest of 'ee?'

HARDY'S HEART (II)

There is odd folklore attaching to the above episode, which also circulates merrily in local public houses.

Hardy's heart was removed, at his home Max Gate, by his personal physician, Dr E. Mann and his surgeon partner Dr Nash-Wortham. What happened to it thereafter is the subject of apocryphal tale-telling so often repeated, and so authoritatively, as to be widely accepted as fact.

According to one current version of the legend, Hardy's ticker was stored overnight in a biscuit tin, deposited in the garden shed. The household cat (Cobweb) got access to it, and ate what she quite reasonably took to be unwanted offal. One variant then has it that the cat (containing the heart of the country's greatest author) was discovered next morning by the undertaker, who working out what had happened wrung its neck (before presumably it could excrete its ill-gotten feast) and placed the feline corpse in the casket due to be buried. Dead Cobweb was ceremonially laid to rest at Stinsford (the congregation and Great British Public being none the wiser), while the identical casket, containing Hardy's ashes, was interred, simultaneously, in the Abbey.

Another version has it that the Stinsford casket was deposited empty into the grave, while Cobweb dropped the digested heart who knows where. Like Alexander's noble ashes, Hardy's decomposed heart may have ended up as so much dirt 'stopping a bung

Symbolic Burials

The novelist Ayn Rand, whose fiction was an inspiration both for Reagonomics, and the economic philosophy of Alan Greenspan, was buried under a gigantic floral wreath in the shape of a \$. The ashes of Harold Robbins (lifetime sales, 750 million, and lots of dollars) are interred, in Palm Springs, in an urn in the form of one of his bestselling books (a carpet bag might, perhaps, have been more appropriate).

The Victorian novelist M.P. Shiel (author of such

hole' in public houses where local people were still chortling over 'where be the rest of 'ee?'

It's not true, as stalwarts of the Hardy Society who have investigated the story assert. What cat, they ask, is big enough to eat a human heart; assuming that such a feline possessed sufficient safe-breaker skills to prise the lid off a biscuit tin in the first place? Moreover the Max Gate cat, Cobweb, survived its master by some years. Possibly one of those mysterious pumas, glimpsed from time to time in the English countryside, may have been roaming Wessex and stopped by the shed for a midnight snack. But there is no report of any such in the local papers.

Ever resourceful, and ever disinclined to lose a good story, the legend gets round this by varying the story to make it a dog and a bowl. Though, of course, a dog would be too big for the burial casket.

The final disproof of the cat-ate-the-heart story came in the 1960s, when the biscuit tin in question resurfaced, along with a much-misspelled note by the then Max Gate gardener, Bertie, testifying that the receptacle had indeed contained the writer's

xenophobic classics as *The Yellow Danger*, 1898) left his ashes
to his disciple, John Gawsworth, who reportedly preserved
them in a biscuit tin (how useful those things were) on his
mantelpiece. Favoured guests would have a pinch of the
Shiel ashes dropped into their stew. Barry Humphries, who
describes Gawsworth as a poet 'who was out of fashion
before he was born' was favoured with a dish of the Shiel
stew. As he says, 'I had a little taste.' He thus qualifies as
the only living literary cannibal. But as he says, 'out of polite-
ness', not relish for the dish.

organ overnight. There are blood stains still very evident on the
tin (the last traces of Hardy's DNA extant, the Hardy Society
notes, with a wild hope that, in some Jurassic literary park of the
future, a cloned Hardy might be possible).

There is a last telling detail:

> the manufacturer's name stamped into the base [of the biscuit tin]
> is no longer legible; but still quite colourfully and even garishly present
> on the top and sides are several images of kittens, including one in
> which they are depicted in the process of catching and presumably
> killing a bird with the somewhat ironic caption, 'In disgrace'.

The ironies would, one suspects, have pleased Hardy immensely.
When he came into the world, the midwife assumed he was dead,
and put the little body aside, as still-born. He was born a corpse,
and ended cat's meat – ashes and biscuit tins: a fitting end for
the greatest ironist of his age.

See, for instance, his poem, 'In the Cemetery':

'You see those mothers squabbling there?'
Remarks the man of the cemetery.
'One says in tears, "'Tis mine lies here!"
Another, "Nay, mine, you Pharisee!"
Another, "How dare you move my flowers
And put your own on this grave of ours!"
But all their children were laid therein
At different times, like sprats in a tin.
'And then the main drain had to cross,
And we moved the lot some nights ago,
And packed them away in the general foss
With hundreds more. But their folks don't know,
And as well cry over a new-laid drain
As anything else, to ease your pain!'

CAN WE CLONE DICKENS?

Wednesday 8 June 1870 was the last full day of Charles Dickens's life. He was at home, in Gad's Hill. The Kent countryside 'was delicious with the foliage and flowers of early summer'. He started the day in matching mood, and set to work on his novel in progress, *The Mystery of Edwin Drood*. He was fifty-eight years old, and writing (and selling) better than ever.

Dickens wrote for a few hours. His last words (on paper) record, with poignant vivacity, the light, scents and birdsong streaming in through the open windows in his work-chalet, the annexe to the main house where he liked to write. The novelist then relaxed with a cigar in his newly built conservatory, of which he was very proud. He then took care of some correspondence in his library, before joining his daughter, Georgina, for an informal dinner *à deux*. She noticed as he sat at the dining room table, that her father did not look well, and asked was he ill? Let Peter Ackroyd pick up the story from here:

> Then something happened. He experienced some kind of fit against which he tried to struggle – he paused for a moment and then began to talk very quickly and indistinctly . . . Georgina rose from her chair, alarmed and told him 'to come and lie down'.
> 'Yes', he said, 'On the ground.'
> But as she helped him he slid from her arms and fell heavily to the floor. He was now unconscious.

He would never regain consciousness. Nor would posterity ever know how *Drood* was meant to end. It would, true to its title, remain a mystery.

Someone, perhaps Georgina or his manservant, removed Dickens's collar as he lay writhing on the floor or the adjoining sofa. That was standard first aid with someone experiencing a fit – as was putting a wooden clothes-peg between the sufferer's teeth, lest they bite their tongue off.

It was common in Victorian England for gentlemen to have detachable collars attached by two studs: the collars could be changed daily, the shirt weekly, thus saving on the expense of laundry. And clothes-pegs.

Dickens may not, in fact (since he was at home), have changed his collar that day. He almost certainly did not dress for dinner. We can deduce these domestic facts because that fatal collar came up for sale at Sotheby's a few years ago. It was described in the firm's catalogue as 'soiled', and indeed it was. (I saw it, through a friend at the New Bond Street auctioneers, with my own eyes. I also touched it, with the reverence of an early Christian reaching for the robe of his saviour.)

A dirty collar is of no relevance to genius. Except that the sweat, seeped into the starched cotton, would, surely, still contain the Dickensian DNA. Would it not be possible for science (*Jurassic Park*-style), by means of this precious bodily fluid, to *clone* Charles Dickens: imitate that is, the 'Great Inimitable'? Please, yes.

3
Tools of the Trade

'I love being a writer, what I can't stand is the paperwork.'

Peter De Vries

'Set it Down':
But How Exactly?

After his first brush with the ghost, his father and late King of Denmark, on the battlements of Elsinore, Hamlet says (exploding with rage against his fratricidal, incestuous, adulterous uncle-father Claudius, new King of Denmark):

> O villain, villain, smiling, damned villain!
> My tables! Meet it is I set it down
> That one may smile, and smile, and be a villain;
> At least I am sure it may be so in Denmark.
> So, uncle, there you are.

Most editions add the stage instruction (not Shakespearian, of course): 'He writes'.

Why does Hamlet write? What does he write on? What does he write with? And what does he write? And, last question, does he write at all?

In performance – at a crisis in the action – the episode is deadly and defies most actors' powers to keep the dramatic momentum going. A young man, at the midnight hour, has seen a ghost. His hair is standing on end with shock, like the quills of the fretful porpentine. And what does this young man do? He fishes in his doublet pocket for a notebook (i.e., 'tables', or 'writing tablet') and jots down a memorandum. Can one imagine Jamie Lee Curtis, pausing in her midnight flight from Michael Myers's slashing knife, to make a note to herself in *Halloween*?

Actors, from Garrick onwards (who plausibly assumed a missing 'anon', or 'later' after 'set it down') believe the pedantic

49

instruction 'he writes' is textually wrong, as well as grossly un-theatrical. What is meant here, they suggest, is something along the lines of 'Gosh! A man may smile and nonetheless be a villain. I really ought to write that down sometime, when I have a moment or two to spare.' The observation in question is, of course, banal in the extreme.

If, as most commentators and editors insist, Hamlet *does* write, why, having just come face to face with a revenant from purga-tory (something, incidentally, which proves the rightness of Catholic cosmology – a very big thing) would he choose to inscribe the 'villain-smile' platitude, rather than 'GOD EXISTS!!!!!' We assume his 'tables' are a commonplace book in which he puts down observations, later to be burnished into witty epigrams.

Theorists of the notorious 'delay' in killing Claudius see the business with the 'tables' as highly significant. Hamlet is a 'student', not a 'revenger'. On being told his uncle has debauched his mother, poisoned his father, popped in between him (young Hamlet) and the crown, he doesn't whip out his bare bodkin and do it pat. He whips out his pen and jots down one of the less interesting things the ghost said, in passing, about human nature. The revenge of the nerd will be a long time coming. If ever.

I say pen, but what exactly does Hamlet write with, and on?

Scholars, recently, have become very interested in this ques-tion. There is general agreement that the 'tables' would be a wood, or card-covered pocketbook: probably with only two, replaceable, facing sheets. There could be a stylus (with soft-metalled lead tip) clipped on to the back board.

Hamlet is a young student, up with the latest tools of the student trade. It would be nice to think that attached to the 'tables', by string, would be one of the newfangled 'lead' pencils that had just been devised. A few decades before the putative date of *Hamlet* as the historians of the pencil tell us:

a deposit of graphite (pure black carbon) was found at Borrowdale in Cumbria, in a form so solid and uniform that it could be sawn into sheets and then cut into thin square sticks ... Little chemistry was known in 1564, so the material was called plumbago, or that which acts (writes) like lead.

Original pencils, as explained, would have slices, not a central circular core of 'lead'. And the slice would have been clamped, like Kraft cheese in a sandwich, between planed wood.

It is hard to believe that a London-based author, like Shakespeare, obliged to make hasty corrections to his playscripts, would not know about the new pencil-thing. Nor, as I say, that a smart young university student, like Hamlet, wouldn't see the attractiveness of it for catching ideas as they fizzed up in the brain and were meet to put down.

The First
Typewriter-Writer

Mark Twain asserts, in 1905, in his essay 'The First Typing Machine' that the first such writer/typewriter was none other than Mark Twain:

I will now claim – until dispossessed – that I was the first person in the world to apply the type-machine to literature. That book must have been *The Adventures of Tom Sawyer*.

As Darren Wershler-Henry points out in his history of literary typewriting, this may be what Huck Finn would call a bit of a 'stretcher'. The evidence of the literary remains indicates that it was not *Sawyer* (1876) but the much later *Life on the Mississippi* (1883).

This later date puts Mark Twain in second place, some months behind another famous name. In 1882, for the sum of 375 marks, Friedrich Nietzsche acquired a Hansen 'writing ball', or '*schreibkügel*'. Hansen was a Swedish pastor and teacher of deaf-mutes. He intended his invention as an aid for these unfortunates, not German philosophers of stern persuasion.

On his new writing toy, Nietzsche (type)wrote:

THE WRITING BALL IS A THING LIKE ME: MADE
OF IRON
YET EASILY TWISTED ON JOURNEYS.
PATIENCE AND TACT ARE REQUIRED IN ABUN-
DANCE,
AS WELL AS FINE FINGERS, TO USE US.

Thus typed Zarathustra. He did not have fingers sufficiently fine, or the necessary patience and tact, Nietzsche decided, and returned to his old writing utensils.

JACK VERSUS BLICK

No one could accuse Jack London of being in any sense disabled. He ranks as the most magnificently abled writer in American literature. None the less, as he recalls in his 'alcoholic memoirs', *John Barleycorn*, his inauguration in the writing profession, with the dubious aid of his first typewriter, was one of the hardest struggles of his life: harder, almost, than tramping across the snowy wastes of the Yukon in search of gold.

It was during his freshman year at Berkeley in 1897 that, as London recalls, he 'resolved to write'. And write Jack did – heroically:

> On occasion I composed steadily, day after day, for fifteen hours a day. At times I forgot to eat, or refused to tear myself away from my passionate outpouring in order to eat. And then there was the matter of typewriting. My brother-in-law owned a machine which he used in the day-time. In the night I was free to use it ... It must have been a first model in the year one of the type-writer era. Its alphabet was all capitals ... I had to hit the keys so hard that I strained my first fingers to the elbows, while the ends of my fingers were blisters burst and blistered again.

The diabolic machine, which took Jack (a lover of fisticuffs) to the full, exhausting, fifteen rounds, was a 'Blick', the invention of George Blickensderfer. London's supposition that it was a pioneer machine is correct. The firm brought out the 'first truly portable typewriter' in 1893. It was, by all accounts, a hostile beast. Few got an easy victory over Herr Blick.

Historians of the typewriter none the less admire the machine because, although Blickensderfer could never exploit the poten-tial, it is the forerunner of the IBM Selectric 'golfball'. Unfortunately, coming on the scene as it did long before its tech-nological moment, the Blick was fatally clunky and prone to jam, as London bitterly complains.

None of London's Blick-work made it into print (nor would anything he wrote, until he returned from the frozen north a year later). But he can be said to have beaten the machine. He can claim to be a slow-typing world champion.

Famous Writers' Typewriters

If there was a golden typewriter award, for the machine whose rollers have generated most high-grade literature, Remington would win it hands down. Their portables were used by George Orwell, Agatha Christie and Tennessee Williams. William Faulkner favoured the desk-sized Remington.

Other writers' trusty machines include:

Hunter S. Thompson: the IBM Selectric. When blocked, he would shoot it with his other favourite tool, the handgun.

Ernest Hemingway and P.G Wodehouse: the 'Royal' portable.

Ian Fleming also favoured the 'Royal'. He went even more royal by having his machine plated with gold. It was sold for £56,250 (US$89,229) at Christie's in 1995. It is not recorded whether it was purchased by a sinister German with plans to raid Fort Knox and a personal attendant called Oddjob.

Thanks to the mytypewriter.com website for this wholly pointless information.

THE COMPUTERISED NOVEL

The first novelist to attract publicity for his use of the newfangled computer-thing was the thriller writer Desmond Bagley, in the 1970s. So ignorant were the public and journalists that there was a general misapprehension that – somehow – Bagley's computer was actually writing his books.

Bagley, who died in 1983, is deeply sunk into oblivion. The loyal website, www.desmondbagley.co.uk (little competition for that URL, one suspects) carries the forlorn announcement:

> 12 April 2007: Today saw the twenty-fourth anniversary of Desmond Bagley's passing. The hit-rate for this web-site seems to be declining rapidly. Hardly surprising really as there is no-one publishing the novels at the moment. House of Stratus, who offered print-on-demand editions of the entire catalogue, have ceased trading.

Despite this cyber-gloom, Desmond deserves some small commemoration for compositorial innovation.

It was Arthur C. Clarke, a novelist whose finger was always resting on the pulse of the future, who was the trail-blazing digital pioneer. In 1978, Clarke (then sixty) announced his retirement. He was not in good health, and the sheer labour of writing was increasingly beyond him.

Clarke was sucked back into fiction by a software program. Micropro's WordStar, released in 1979, was the first widely available word processing package and was, by the mid-1980s, the industry standard. Clarke prominently acknowledged the co-authorial assistance of WordStar in his novels of his early 1980s renaissance. Beautifully named, WordStar (the WP system I started on) required mastering some clunky codes, and interfacing with printers was tricky. But, once mastered, the prose could flow with an ease no typewriter or pen and yellow pad could rival. One slid, as effortlessly as a figure skater, over the screen.

In 1982, Clarke published a sequel to his bestselling *2001: A Space Odyssey*, entitled, unadventurously, *2010: Odyssey Two*. This, like its Kubrick-directed predecessor, was adapted for cinema. As with Kubrick, Clarke was a valued adviser and he worked closely with film's director, Peter Hyams. They used 'Kaypro' computers and a telephone modem: Clarke being resident (as he had been for years) in Sri Lanka and Hyams in Los Angeles.

The Kaypro, like Adam Osborne's pioneering machine, was a 'luggable'. The size of a small suitcase and weighing some thirty pounds, they represented the first generation of computers which broke away from fixed, desktop, immobility. They boasted up to 64K Ram and a 9-inch screen. Big deal. Then.

Portable they indisputably were. But not easily portable. The Kaypro (like the Zorba, and unlike IBM's 'Peanut') was encased in heavy metal which protected it from jarring, but did nothing for ease of carriage. Or beauty. But, by God, we who had them (in my case the Zorba – which I never booted up without thinking of 'the Greek') felt cutting edge. Or lugging edge.

The proprietor of Micropro, the company whose WordStar had brought Clarke back into active writing life, was Seymour Rubinstein. A keen reader of SF, Rubinstein asked Clarke what he foresaw for the computer. Clarke, presciently, prophesied brief-case-sized machines which could communicate, in super-modem links, with each other all over the world.

The prophecy should be taken in context with predictions by industry 'insiders' – hard-headed fellows, who despised SF fanta-sists, like the author of *The Sands of Mars*. The magazine *Popular*

Mechanics, for example, solemnly predicted in 1949 'Computers in the future may weigh no more than 1.5 tons.' Thank God for that. Ten years later, Thomas Watson, the chairman of IBM, chanced his arm with the estimate: 'I think there is a world market for maybe five computers.'

Clarke was right about the laptop and almost right about the Internet. Interestingly, Clarke latterly voiced some distaste for the World Wide Web. Like trying to fill up a glass of water from Niagara, he thought.

Literary Landfills

When Edmund Spenser died in 1599, and was buried in Poets' Corner, legend has it that assembled round his coffin as it was lowered to its resting place were the leading play-wrights of the time: Jonson, Beaumont, Fletcher and Shakespeare. As tribute, they threw manuscript elegies into the earth, along with their quills. As landfills go, it is hard to think of a finer literary dump. Nor can one imagine a similarly distinguished band of contemporary authors hurling their laptops and elegiac floppies into the grave, to accompany one of their number to eternity. In 1938 what was assumed to be Spenser's resting place was dug up, in the hope of finding that unicorn among literary relics, the holograph manuscript of a Shakespeare work. Alas, 'all that was discovered was a collapsed lead coffin surrounded by dry soil'.

SERVING THE WRITER

Carlyle was eloquent on the necessity in society of what he called 'servantship' – the complement to his ideal of hero-worship. Servants were also necessary to the writing life. Famously, Carlyle had some unfortunate experiences with these human tools of the author's trade.

In the mid-1830s he and his wife Jane had come down to London from Craigenputtock to make Thomas's fortune in the literary world. In London, he was encouraged by John Stuart Mill in his great project, a history of the French Revolution. Ten years the younger man, Mill had been a child prodigy and was by now an eminent philosopher. He could help a struggling sage.

In early March (typically a cold month in England – this detail is important) Carlyle asked Mill if he would comment on the manuscript of the first volume (of three) of his great work. It was some 260 pages long, and his only copy.

A response came quickly. On the evening of 6 March, a hand knocked on the door of the Carlyles' house in Cheyne Walk. It was Mill, horribly distraught and practically inarticulate. There had been a disaster. A housemaid (some accounts add the epithet 'illiterate') had mistaken Carlyle's manuscript for kindling and had burned all but four or five sheets. It is not recorded whether Mill brought the singed relics with him.

It was not entirely the maid's fault. Mill admitted that the manuscript had been 'left out by him in too careless a manner'. Not a pleasing detail. None the less, Carlyle took it like a man. He wrote to his wife: 'Mill, poor fellow, is terribly cut up. We must endeavour to hide from him how very serious this business is for us.'

It was indeed very serious. Carlyle had been working on the

French Revolution project for half a year without financial support. Everything was riding on this book's success. And, temporarily, as such things do, the calamity knocked the stuffing out of him. He felt like a man who had 'nearly killed himself accomplishing zero'.

Mill offered £200 in compensation. At first Carlyle refused, but eventually accepted £100 for his time and a new (and, as he jested, less combustible) stock of writing paper. He was, after all, a Scot.

Carlyle recovered his energies and *The French Revolution* was published to huge success, two years later. All turned out well. There remain, however, some curious aspects to the affair. The maid would not, surely, have needed 260 pages as kindling. You could have started the Great Fire of London with that much paper.

Paper, anyway, would not be incinerated carelessly. In a well-regulated household like the Mills', fine-quality writing paper would be recycled for wadding, or for the privies (the servants' if not the family's). That particular fate would have been even harder to explain to Carlyle than the flames, perhaps.

Could it even – in some infection of revolutionary spirit among the servant class – have been done maliciously?

Curious too is what happened to the maid. The Mills were notoriously soft-hearted. The Carlyles, less so. Particularly where servant morals came into it.

As Alison Light recalls in *Mrs Woolf and the Servants*, sometime after the event:

> Jane Carlyle belatedly discovered that a hapless maid had given birth in the china closet and kept it secret. The master had been entertaining a guest in the dining room at the time with 'just a thin small door between!' Mrs Carlyle made a wry joke of it in her correspondence but the 'creature' was instantly sent packing.

For the idle mind it is irresistible to fantasise that the anonymous maid of the Mills knew about the savagery of the Carlyles against her class and was striking a blow for a fellow underling against those Scottish puritans in Cheyne Walk.

4

Sex and the Victorians

'If all hearts were open and all desires known – as they would
be if people showed their souls – how many gapings, sighings,
clenched fists, knotted brows, broad grins, and red eyes should we
see in the market-place!'

Thomas Hardy

First-Night Nerves

In early 2007, a monograph was published by Helena Michie entitled: *Victorian Honeymoons: Journeys to the Conjugal*. Learned monographs rarely excite even the learned. But the topic was fascinating, and – as often happens – oddly topical. The best-selling 'literary' novel of the day, jogging along, week by week, in the top ten was *On Chesil Beach*.

If one credits the work's author, Ian McEwan, the Victorian honeymoon long outlasted the Victorian era. It lasted until July 1962, to be precise, six months before Philip Larkin recorded the age of sexual intercourse as beginning with his much quoted lines from 'Annus Mirabilis':

> Sexual intercourse began
> In nineteen sixty-three
> (Which was rather late for me) –

As it proved for the lugubrious poet (writing in June 1967), it is 'too late' for the twenty-two-year-old principals of *On Chesil Beach*. McEwan's novel opens:

> They were young, educated, and both virgins on this, their wedding night, and they lived in a time when a conversation about sexual difficulties was plainly impossible.

There follows what may be the most microscopically described wedding night in contemporary fiction. A lone pubic hair dangling from the bride's panties is given the kind of attention devoted by Elizabethan sonneteers to my lady's eyebrow. The outcome is disastrous. The morning after finds the couple 'both virgins'.

Edward and Florence, McEwan's newly-weds, are graduates of metropolitan institutions and, by the standards of 1962, worldly. Hotels hold no terrors for them, hotel bedrooms do. They are, we understand, children of the time: and the time is sexually hung-up. They, particularly the bride, are as cripplingly inhibited as the newly-weds Marie Stopes described in *Married Love* in 1918:

> When the wife discovers the true nature of his body, and learns the part she has to play as a wife, she may refuse utterly to agree to her husband's wishes. There have been not a few brides whom the horror of the first night of marriage with a man less considerate has driven to suicide or insanity.

If Ian McEwan was more gothically inclined he might have subtitled *On Chesil Beach* something like *The Horror of the First Night of Marriage* (McEwan's actual title alludes to Matthew Arnold's honeymoon poem, 'Dover Beach').

There was more marrying in the early 1960s than today – another Victorian hangover. As one who, in 1962, unlike McEwan, was among that marrying, twenty-something, newly graduated cohort, I have to say that the mutual sexual ignorance (not to say stark virginality) of Edward and Florence presented as something universal among my class of person is unconvincing. But fiction is fiction and writes its own histories.

And who, ultimately, can say? As Helena Michie observes, since the eighteenth century the bedroom door has been firmly slammed on what happens on the wedding night. No bloodstained sheets are hung out nowadays even, one imagines, in rural Italy, where, one is told, the practice held out longest. And even where there are peeps through the bedroom keyhole, it pays to be sceptical.

A famous Victorian case preoccupies Michie. As it happens, much is 'known' about what happened sexually on the wedding night of John and Effie Ruskin in 1848. Nothing happened. End of story. But do we in fact 'know' that? The main evidence is the wife's subsequent explanation to the court, at which she pleaded for annulment of the union, as to why the marriage was never consummated. After many months, her husband 'finally told me the true reason . . . that he had imagined women were quite different from what he saw I was and that the reason he did not make me his wife was because he was disgusted with my person this the first evening 10 April.'

It has been widely assumed that (as the Ruskinist Mary Lutyens put it): 'what disgusted John about Effie's body was probably her pubic hair'. But is this entirely plausible in a much-travelled art historian, close on thirty, who had surely witnessed innumerable life classes at various art schools? The argument is sometimes bolstered with the hypothesis that Effie may have been menstruating. Lyndall Gordon, in her biography of T.S. Eliot suggests something similar happened on the equally disastrous honeymoon of the poet and his first wife, Vivienne. The hint is built on in Michael Hastings' play, *Tom and Viv*. Biographers speculate and playwrights fantasise – but who really knows? Or will ever know? Or has any right to know?

Was John, as apologists like the critic Phyllis Rose suggest, the victim of transient 'honeymooner's embarrassment'? The Ruskins' plight, Rose asserts, 'was probably less extraordinary and eccentric than one might think at first'. As with Stopes's case, a little 'chivalry' and patience could have sorted things out without the lawyers being called in, and Ruskin vilified for ever as art-history's eunuch in chief.

The conclusion Michie comes to about the Ruskins, man and wife (or perhaps not), is that one will never know definitively. It remains a 'mystery story'. Or, as we say in this book, a 'curiosity'.

THE CARLYLES'
WEDDING NIGHT

Popular literary lore has it that Thomas and Jane Welsh Carlyle's wedding night in 1826 was as total a debacle as that of John and Effie Ruskin. There are two main sources. One was Jane's *confidante*, the novelist Geraldine Jewsbury. The honeymoon (so to call it) was spent in 21 Comely Bank, a small house on the edge of Edinburgh. It is not a beautiful quarter of that otherwise beautiful city. According to Jewsbury, on the first morning of marriage, as Jane later confided, Carlyle spent the morning furiously tearing up flowers in the garden. The symbolism was obvious. All pl*ck and no f*ck.

The other source was the literary rogue, Frank Harris. Harris claimed to have had an unbuttoned smoking-room conversation with the eminent physician, Sir Richard Quain, who examined Jane in late life and having made an internal investigation of her was led to expostulate, in amazement 'Why! You're virgo intacta.' Thereafter Jane (the most modest of women, as Sir Richard was among the most discreet and respectable of Victorian doctors) reportedly confided that on the wedding night Thomas, beneath the sheets, had done things to himself – 'jiggling like'.

Sir Richard (as Harris claimed) understood perfectly: 'the poor devil in a blue funk was frigging himself'. Quain's alleged remarks were elaborated, in later years, in a version which proposed that Jane's lifelong hymeneal intactness was established when her corpse was taken to London's St George's Hospital after her death in 1866 and subjected to post-mortem examination.

One of Carlyle's doughtiest, and most indignant, defenders, Sir James Crichton-Browne, followed up these claims (Harris's is, prima facie, preposterous) in 1903, with some enterprising legwork. The house at 21 Comely Bank, he established, had no garden and since the wedding took place on 17 October, there would have been no flowers to tear up. Case closed.

Sir Richard Quain was unavailable for interview. But Crichton-Browne discovered the attending house-surgeon at St George's Hospital on the date in question, a Dr Ridge-Jones, and established there was no examination made, nor was there any coroner's inquest on Mrs Carlyle's body. Case closed. Bedroom door even more firmly closed.

All victims of scandalous gossip should have their Crichton-Browne.

DOROTHEA'S WEDDING NIGHT

The most famous wedding night in classic literary fiction is that in *Middlemarch*, 'the primal scene of fictional honeymoons', as Helena Michie (see p. 63) grandly calls it in her treatise on 'conjugal journeying'. In the novel, George Eliot skips over Dorothea Brooke's actual experience in the brusquest of sentences. Not long after the dinner party, described in chapter 10, we are told, 'Dorothea had become Mrs Casaubon and was on her way to Rome.' What, one may speculate, does 'become' mean here? Is more than name-change involved? Has the 'maiden' become a 'wife' – as Mrs Ruskin never did on the fateful night of 10 April 1848?

There followed, for the first readers, a two-month and ten-chapter gap between the 'books' of the serially published novel. In chapter 20, the narrative jumps forward to Dorothea, now a married lady, in the boudoir of a handsome apartment in the Via

The Other Bedroom Problem

Heroic literary insomniacs have, as their patron saint, John of the Cross, who composed his poems in what he called the 'dark night of the soul'.

Other dark night sufferers and soulful celebrators of insomnia, include:

Gerard Manley Hopkins (viz: 'I wake and feel the fell of dark, not day').

Chaucer (viz: 'As I lay in my bed sleep full unmet').

Dante Gabriel Rossetti (viz: his poem 'Insomnia', which helped put the word into everyday parlance).

Stephen King (viz: his novel *Insomnia* – gothic improbability apart, a useful guide to off-the-shelf and prescription remedies).

Mark Twain was a famous insomniac: often, in the agony

Sistina. She is 'sobbing bitterly'. Mr Casaubon is in the Vatican (among congenial celibates, we apprehend). Dorothea, we are told, has 'no distinctly shapen grievance'. It is, apparently, the 'stupendous fragmentariness' of Rome which has 'heightened the dreamlike strangeness of her bridal life' and brought her to this tearful condition.

Even in someone as finely tuned to experience as Dorothea,

insomnia, he would leave his bed to sleep on the bathroom floor.

Charles Dickens wrote his *Uncommercial Traveller* sketches (all seventeen of them), and the famous death scene of Jo the sweeper (*Bleak House*) during bouts of insomnia and restless leg syndrome. The so-called 'dark phase' of his later career suggests chronic sleeplessness.

Franz Kafka (unsurprisingly, given the sleeplessness of his victim heroes) was a lifelong insomniac. After an hour's restless slumber, he would wake up, he said, 'as though I had laid my head in the wrong hole' – a remark which the vulgar might misconstrue.

The poet Amy Lowell was in the practice of renting five rooms in any hotel she booked into, so as to create quiet above, below, and on either side. Few poets have been well-heeled enough to afford more than the proverbial (noisy) garret.

it is hard to credit that it is the 'gigantic broken revelations of that Imperial and Papal city' which have reduced her to this tempestuous weeping. Is she, not to mince words, still intact?

That Casaubon has not been up to his wedding-night task is the received opinion. Judicious as ever, Michie weighs the evidence and concludes differently:

While critics have long assumed that Casaubon was impotent and
the Casaubon marriage unconsummated, his preoccupation with
'forms' suggests to me a rigid adherence to conjugal duty.

In support of her assumption that intercourse, if only of a
'formal' nature, took place, and was experienced by Dorothea as
horrific molestation, Michie reads her phantasmagoric recoil from
Rome's stupendous fragmentariness as 'sounding very like the
horrifying and repetitive dreams of rape survivors'. The Stopesian
horror of the wedding night, again.

This may be a reading too far. It is, with the best will in the
world, difficult to picture the Rev. Edward Casaubon as a ravishing
Tarquin. But I think Michie's assumption is essentially correct.
Something sexual happened in the Via Sistina. The subject
inevitably tempts one to prurience and ingenuity. There has always
seemed to me a broad hint (allusive in this instance, not metaphor-
ical) in the epigraph to chapter 21:

> Hir facounde eke full womanly and plain,
> No contrefeted termes had she
> To semen wise.[*]

The chapter itself picks up on the earlier description of Dorothea's
sobbing. Ladislaw has come to visit. This is their first intimate
encounter and may, plausibly, be seen as the moment when their
relationship begins: a relationship which will culminate in a second,
happier, honeymoon for Dorothea.

George Eliot gave careful thought to her epigraphs – sometimes, when one could not be found in her commonplace books
or memory, she would fake them up herself in effectively antique

[*] glossary: 'fauconde' = 'demeanour'; 'contrefeted termes' = 'counterfeited, fake turn of
speech'; 'semen' = 'seem, make herself appear'

styles. This we are merely told, is 'Chaucer'. It is, annotation informs us (few, other than medievalists, will be able identify the lines unaided), from one of the less read parts of *The Canterbury Tales*, 'The Physician's Tale'.

Brief, and undistinguished by comparison with the better-known tales, it tells the story of the delectable fourteen-year-old Virginia, coveted by the lecherous judge Apius in Ancient Rome. Rather than surrender her maidenhood, Virginia consents to have her head cut off. She dies a vestal.

On the face of it, this would seem to support the interpretation that Dorothea is still a virgin in Rome, and may indeed have put up a struggle to preserve her virginity (like McEwan's Florence) on the wedding night. There is, however, an opposite inference to be drawn from the epigraph. It is inconceivable that Eliot, the consort of the leading popular scientist of the age, was not aware of the resonances of Chaucer's word 'semen' to the modern ear and that she could not, had she wanted, have chosen some other passage or spelling. Dorothea, the hint implies, has carnal knowledge, she is semen-wise. Weighed carefully (too carefully perhaps) the balance of evidence supports Michie.

George Eliot's Two Honeymoons

Like Dorothea, Eliot herself experienced two honeymoons: one blissful, one nightmarish. The first, unsolemnised by church ceremony, was with G(eorge) H(enry) Lewes, probably in 1853, as her biographer Rosemary Ashton records. The novelist was thirty-five, and now happier, as she told a close friend, than in 'most years of my life'.

Eliot's second marriage, aged sixty and now a widow, to her disciple, John W. Cross, twenty years her junior, resulted in a honeymoon of more than Ruskinian awfulness. During the wedding trip in Venice, Cross, as Rosemary Ashton recounts, 'suffered some kind of fit or derangement. He jumped from their hotel room into the Grand Canal.'

It was, in all probability, a suicide attempt. According to one rumour, the newly-wed husband 'begged the gondoliers not to rescue him'. As Ashton concludes, sagely, 'Inevitably, perhaps, the marriage, the honeymoon, and the canal incident attracted gossip of this kind, which can in the nature of things be neither fully confirmed nor fully discounted.' But, as Michie's interesting book, and one's own curiosity on the subject, demonstrate, the urge to confirm or discount – to 'pry' in a word – is as irresistible as it is ultimately unsatisfiable.

THE LANGUAGE OF FLOWERS

The most hilariously impossible flowers in literature are found in chapter 8 ('The Queen's Croquet Ground') in *Alice in Wonderland* where the young heroine comes on three playing-card gardeners painting white roses red at the command of the Queen of Hearts (nothing but red for her).

Another wholly fantastic bloom, horticulturalists tell us, is the fabled black tulip, about which Alexandre Dumas wrote his tulipo-mania romance in 1850. Is Oscar Wilde's trademark green carnation as artificial as the mad Queen's red roses or as impossible as Dumas's *Tulipa negra*?

In 1894 the young man of letters, Robert Hichens brought out a mischievously satirical novel called *The Green Carnation*. It was published anonymously with a thinly pseudonymised Oscar Wilde, as 'Esmé Amarinth' and his lover, Lord Alfred Douglas as 'Lord Reggie Hastings'. The name Amarinth (i.e. the flower Amaranth) was evidently chosen carefully and spitefully.

Hichens's narrative opens with the dandy, Reggie, narcissistically ornamenting himself:

> He slipped a green carnation into his evening coat, fixed it in its place with a pin, and looked at himself in the glass, the long glass that stood near the window of his London bedroom.

The rumour swept round London that Oscar himself was the author of the novel named after his trademark buttonhole. *The Green Carnation* – floral artifice and work of fiction – was an exquisite joke on the dull world, to be appreciated only by green-carnationed insiders.

Wilde was irritated by the rumour and wrote a public letter to the *Pall Mall Gazette*, in which he asserted 'I invented that wonderful flower' but 'with the middle-class and mediocre book that usurps its strangely beautiful name I have, I need hardly say, nothing to do. The flower is a work of art. The book is not.'

The novel was withdrawn from circulation in 1895: not as the result of Wilde's indignation, but in the moral panic which consumed the country during the trials which eventually led to his imprisonment for gross indecency. No green carnations in Reading Gaol.

Did Oscar, as he claims, invent 'that wonderful flower'?

He did not. But he can claim to have invested it with its Masonic significance. The etymological root is in the Latin for 'flesh', as in 'carnal knowledge'. Green, Wilde had declared as early as 1889, is: 'the sign of a subtle artistic temperament, and in nations is said to denote a laxity, if not a decadence, of morals' (it would be a brave fellow who asserted that in a Dublin or Boston pub, on St Patrick's Day to any son of Erin sporting his national colour).

The 'unnatural' flower was a coded hint about a certain kind of sex which the 'earnest', in their ineffable earnestness, nominated 'unnatural'. The green carnation was a *'fleur du mal'*. Baudelairians (au fait with their author's masterwork of decadent verse, 'the flowers of evil') could decode its symbolism with no trouble at all.

Victorian florists might have more trouble supplying the blooms. According to Neil McKenna's *The Secret Life of Oscar Wilde*, Parisian homosexuals had begun wearing artificially dyed green carnations in 1891. Creating them was a tricky process. It was at the hugely successful premiere of *Lady Windermere's Fan* in February 1892, that Wilde (who visited Paris regularly) arranged, as a publicity stunt, for appropriate male members of the audience to wear the talismanic flower.

When asked, subsequently, what the carnation 'meant', Wilde replied, riddlingly: 'Nothing whatever, but that is just what nobody will guess.' Gays and homophobes guessed easily enough, as the last lines of Noël Coward's ditty 'Pretty boys, witty boys' in the 1929 musical *Bitter Sweet*, made clear:

> For the nineties being gay,
> We all wear a green carnation.

GREEN CARNATIONS
(CONTINUED)

The green carnation, as a badge of gay pride continues to be defiantly worn to this day. When, in 2006, Stephen Fry was elected Honorary Patron of the Oscar Wilde Society he sent his fellow members the message:

> Dearest Friends of Oscar – It is November as I write this and I am wearing a red poppy in my lapel. In my heart, however, I wear always a green carnation in honour of Oscar the magnificent, Oscar the glorious, Oscar our friend.

The process by which white carnations became green was, as McKenna explains, pure Queen of Hearts:

> The green carnation . . . is a white carnation, dyed by plunging the stem in an aqueous solution of the aniline dye called malachite green. The dye ascends the petals by capillary attraction, and at the end of twelve hours they are well tinged. A longer immersion deepens the tint.

In Hichens's novel, Amarinth asserts that so beautiful, and logical, is the dyed flower that nature, not to be outdone, will soon recreate it, 'naturally'.

So, in a sense, it eventually happened. The British National Carnations Society website reported in 2006, apropos its Hampton Court summer show – the big day of the year for carnation lovers – that the 'commonest question asked' by the walk-in public was 'Are the green ones dyed?'

The president of the society made clear the brilliant green blooms were not dyed. No illicit 'capillary attraction' was involved:

> Of course as I am sure members will recognise they are Prado a true green. It does however indicate how the general public are unaware of advances in breeding in recent years.

It would be nice to think that the 'unnatural' green carnation became 'natural' in 1967, at the time of the passing of the Sexual Offences Act, which decriminalised the practices for which Oscar was so cruelly sentenced. Alas, it seems to have been slightly later. Art and life never coincide as the author of *The Importance of Being Earnest* would have liked them to.

LOVE MY MANUSCRIPT MORE THAN YOU

US Marines are taught to chant, in witness to their *semper fidelis* oath, 'Love my Rifle More than You'.

Authors sometimes feel the same about their manuscripts.

Dante Gabriel Rossetti's favourite model and the woman to whom he addressed many love poems was Elizabeth Siddal (1829–62). After a decade-long 'open union', Siddal became Mrs Rossetti in 1860. The marriage was short and unhappy. She sank into laudanum addiction and terminal depression after the still-born birth of a daughter. Rossetti, true to his bohemian beliefs ('*semper infidelis*'), was an ostentatiously bad husband. Elizabeth's death may have been suicide. She was in her early thirties, and died still stunningly beautiful.

Siddal's body was laid to rest in Highgate Cemetery.

A remorseful Rossetti enclosed a manuscript copy of his poems in progress in her coffin, nestling them in her famous red tresses, alongside her Bible.

Seven years later, himself now drug-addicted, depressed and blocked, both as painter and poet, Rossetti became obsessed with recovering what was buried in Highgate. Not his wife Lizzie, that is: his manuscript. His agent, Charles Augustus Howell, was prepared to play the grave robber in the interests of great literature (and his commission). On his part Rossetti was friendly with the Home Secretary and, after some private petitioning, the necessary letter of authority to exhume was procured on 28 September 1869.

The deed was done, Frankenstein-style, secretly, at night, by lamplight. A doctor was in attendance, to disinfect the manuscript. Rossetti himself could not bear to be present and the details, possibly false, were passed on to him by Howell. Despite all the parties' desire to keep it secret the story 'oozed out' (as Rossetti's biographer, Jan Marsh, aptly puts it). The coffin, reportedly, emitted a 'dreadful smell' when unsealed. But, despite her years entombed, Siddal was, Howell observed, as beautiful as she had been in life. Her crowning glory, her mane of burning red hair, had grown to fill the coffin. As Marsh says, 'one imagines a rather silent group leaving the cemetery'.

The manuscript volume was unpleasantly damp, Rossetti found, and had a 'great worm hole' through it. Nonetheless, the poems were recovered – most gratefully to posterity the revised version of the dramatic monologue 'Jenny'. It recalls a night-long visit by the poet to a prostitute:

Fair Jenny mine, the thoughtless queen
Of kisses which the blush between
Could hardly make much daintier;
Whose eyes are as blue skies, whose hair
Is countless gold incomparable:
Fresh flower, scarce touched with signs that tell
Of Love's exuberant hotbed.

It seems a curious memento to accompany one's wife on her last journey in her very unexuberant cold bed. But Rossetti was a curious man.

By way of postscript, one may note that Siddal's grave is listed on the London's Haunted Places website. Whether the ghost who haunts it is flaming haired, or bushily bearded, is not recorded. Rossetti's recovery of his manuscript won the April 2007 competition sponsored by http://blogcritics.org for 'The Creepiest Thing Writer's Block Has Caused Someone to Do'.

5

Better Than Sex, Some Say

Yet know I five or six
Smokers who freely mix
Still with their neighbours.
Charles Stuart Calverley, 'Ode to Tobacco' (1862)

THREE CASTLES

The Victorians preferred to lard literary associations, rather than death threats, onto their beloved weed. With this in mind, W.D. & H.O. Wills, the English tobacco firm based in Bristol, then an English port with close sea-links to America, introduced their Three Castles 'Virginia' brand in 1878. According to Wills's house-history:

> This name was adopted as the result of a suggestion by an Edinburgh sealing wax and stationery manufacturer named George Waterston. He was a smoker of Wills's Bird's Eye tobacco, in praise of which he had written several times to the firm. In December 1876 he wrote: 'It has often occurred to me that it would be worthwhile for a Bristol tobacco manufacturer to bring out a first-rate tobacco under the brand of the Three Castles as described by Thackeray in his novel *The Virginians* where he says, "There's no sweeter tobacco comes from Virginia and no better brand than the Three Castles."'

The Virginians is not ranked high among Thackeray's work. The author was not himself over-pleased with this late production: 'the worst novel I ever wrote', he once grumbled. 'The worst novel *anyone* ever wrote,' a friend quipped back. With friends like that, who needs critics?

Set in the revolutionary war, *The Virginians* follows the fortunes of the Warrington twins, born into the plantation-owning, slave-owning, and tobacco-growing classes of southern American gentry. They are descendants of Henry Esmond, the earlier Thackeray hero, whose sword had been drawn for both the

Cigarettes and the Novel

Cigarettes were popularised in Britain (which had hitherto preferred the oriental cheroot) by soldiers returning from the Crimean War in 1855, who had picked up the habit from the Turks. The association with Turkish exoticism was forged – and profitably exploited by the manufacturers. The cigarette was 'sexy', unlike the cigar and pipe, which were merely 'manly'. The first chain-smoking hero in English fiction is Guy Livingstone, in G.A. Lawrence's 1857, ultra 'muscular' novel of that name. Guy is 'vast proportioned but lean in the flanks like a wolf-hound'. And seldom without a cigar between his cruel lips. One of Lawrence's disciples, Ouida, daringly named the gamine heroine 'Cigarette' in her desert romance *Under Two Flags* (1867). Popular as the novel was, the name has never caught on. The cigarette (until recently) did.

Jacobite and Hanoverian causes, and who emigrates to Virginia at the end of the earlier novel.

The novel was serialised 1857–59; the edgy post-*Uncle Tom's Cabin*, pre-Civil War period. Thackeray was hugely popular in America and had visited the country on lucrative lecture tours. He had ten thousand good reasons for favouring the Confederate cause, he liked to jest – meaning that many pounds sterling he had invested in the American South, principally in tobacco. He was himself addicted to the cigar.

Thackeray died, prematurely, in 1863 (smoking alas may have played a part). In the 1870s, he was still a household name. For their Three Castles brand Wills contrived to procure, after extensive negotiation with the novelist's estate, one of the novelist's own designs and the relevant quotation from *The Virginians*. In March 1877, George Wills dispatched an honorary first packet to Mr Waterston. He approved.

Three Castles went on to become a popular brand and (with a redesigned packet, but still sporting Thackeray's encomium) was still being widely smoked as late as the 1960s.

BOND'S BACCY

In 2006 there was hot discussion on the website http://debrief.commanderbond.net as to whether Morland's, the 83 Grosvenor Street tobacconist which custom makes Bond's Balkan Sobranie gaspers, ever actually existed.

The definitive answer was eventually turned up in a small (and itself rather obscure) guidebook to *Goldfinger* by Adrian Turner:

> The shop on Grosvenor Street was tiny and its window display contained bowls of tobacco, smokers' paraphernalia and copies of the latest James Bond novel. Inside, the smell was heavily perfumed and there was always the manager Miss Cohen, a middle-aged woman with glasses and shiny black hair tied in a tight bun. Sometimes you could glimpse a woman in the back room, rolling your very own. Until he became famous, Fleming would visit the shop every week and collect his weekly ration of five hundred at a cost, in 1963, of 37s 6d per hundred.

Despite 007 and his creator's loyal puff, the shop went out of business in the 1970s.

My own (confessedly perfunctory) investigation indicates that the shop's name was derived not from any tobacconist, but a 'Mr William Morland of Grosvenor Street', a tycoon property owner in the area who, in 1792, lent the Prince Regent the money with which to buy Warwick House, adjoining Carlton House which the prince was sumptuously remodelling (he did not want neighbours).

Carlton Cigarettes (introduced in 1913) were a pioneer low-tar brand and Bond would have despised them. His (and his creator's) taste was clearly for something manlier. For Ouida, the cigarette may have come from Venus, for Fleming, it was definitely Mars. In *Thunderball*, the delectable Domino regales 007 with a protracted erotic fantasy about the (heroic) bearded, sailor depicted on the packet of Player's Navy Cut.

When the film of *Thunderball* was released, in 1965, the paperback publishers of the novel, Pan, issued a special celebratory edition, with a pull-out promotional flier for the Player's brand. 'Licensed to kill' would be a nifty inscription to put on the packets nowadays.

MAKE MINE DU MAURIER

The du Mauriers rank as Britain's most distinguished literary, theatre and artistic dynasty: familial proof that genius is hereditary. They did not, however, begin grand. The patriarch George du Maurier (1834–96) was the descendant of a French glass blower, called 'Mathurin'. It was he who assumed the fine sounding 'du Maurier' and propagated the fiction that the family were refugees from the revolutionary tumbrel. They weren't – although the fact was not known, even to Mathurin's direct descendants, until 1962. Two generations of du Mauriers lived and died, happily believing the family myth.

George went on to become the lead cartoonist on *Punch* in the mid-1860s and a distinguished illustrator of English fiction – notably Thackeray. The du Maurier pictorial style was detailed and theatrical in composition, and hit the high-Victorian taste very profitably.

While a twenty-three-year-old art student on the Continent, du Maurier had suddenly lost the sight of his left eye (a shocking experience he was later to use in his own novel, *The Martian*). It was this setback which turned him from painting to graphic work. In the early 1880s, du Maurier's remaining eyesight began to fail. He was friendly at this period with Henry James, whose *Washington Square* (1881) he had sumptuously illustrated. It was du Maurier who suggested to Henry James (who turned the idea down, although his sales were flagging) the melodramatic 'Svengali' scenario that later became du Maurier's most famous work, *Trilby* (this irony is central in David Lodge's 2004 novel, *Author, Author*).

On his side, it was James who suggested to du Maurier that, for the sake of his eyes, he should turn to fiction.

Trilby was popular to the point of mania with the British and American reading publics. A romanticisation of his early days as an English art student in the Latin Quarter of Paris, illustrated by du Maurier himself, the novel showcases a cross-dressing bohemian gamine, Trilby O'Ferrall, and her evil genius, Svengali.

Trilby affected male attire, but nowhere in the novel does she wear the famous hat. That took off with the stage version of the novel, written by Paul Potter, which opened at the Haymarket Theatre in October 1895, earning the actor-manager Beerbohm

Tree so much in box office revenue that he was able to build a new theatre for himself. Du Maurier, who was an innocent in such things, got a measly £75 for the rights.

Tree played Svengali, to great effect, with no restraint on anti-Semitic excess. Pogroms in central Europe had triggered waves of Jewish immigration and the inevitable xenophobia. But the star of the piece was Dorothea Baird. Baird's Trilby is significantly unlike du Maurier's illustration of her in his novel. Baird's *gamin* was barefooted ('Trilby Feet' would become a catchphrase for the fashionably shoeless). She was also a chain-smoker of cigarettes.

Baird's Trilby also sported a wide-brimmed, 'trademark', felt hat. The play triggered a secondary wave of mania even greater than that inspired by the novel. Toulouse Lautrec named his yacht *Trilby*. It became a brand name slapped on innumerable gimcrack products. The music hall stars, Marie Lloyd and Vesta Tilley warbled out songs such as 'Tricky Little Trilby'. Silent film versions followed.

The mania eventually died away (there will, depend on it, come a time when people will say – '*The Da Vinci Code*? Never heard of it'). But the play left behind it a permanent vogue for the Trilby hat. Perhaps in tribute to its bohemian, unrespectable associations the hat was favoured by roguish men. Al Capone's penchant for the trilby, as styled by the Italian firm Borsalino, certified it as the bad guy's ('you looking at me?') fashion statement. Still later, it has been taken up by 'gangsta' rap artists, who would punch your lights out if you dared tell them it was a barefooted woman's hat, and didn't it look sweet?

Du Maurier the Younger:
Cigarettes Again

The author of *Trilby* did not live to reap the full success of his
novel and its adaptations: dramatic, filmic, and sartorial. He died
a year after the novel's publication. His son, Gerald du Maurier
(1873–1934), would go on to be one of the most successful actors
of his time and was knighted in 1922 for services to the stage.
The young man appeared, fittingly, in the Potter-Tree dramatisation
of his father's famous novel.

Gerald's on-stage style was famously suave. According to his
daughter, Daphne du Maurier:

> if an actor approached a scene with too much enthusiasm, Gerald
> would ask, 'Must you kiss her as though you were having steak
> and onions for lunch? It may be what you feel but it's damned
> unattractive from the front row of the stalls. Can't you just say,
> "I love you", and yawn, and light a cigarette and walk away?'

The cigarette was indelibly associated with du Maurier's dinner-
jacketed laid-back style. For generations afterwards, it was said
that British matinee idols simply couldn't act unless they had a
cigarette in one hand, and a tumbler of scotch in the other. It
came to be called 'Geraldism'.

He was, alas, as blasé about paperwork as in his stage image.
In 1929, harassed by the income tax people, du Maurier sold his
name to be used as a brand for the new tipped cigarette, launched
world-wide by the Imperial Tobacco Canada. It was popular from
the first and is still that country's premier brand (the French name

helps in Quebec, like the rappers, they don't care too much about linguistic origins). Du Maurier cigarettes have always appealed to women as much as men – there is a seductiveness in the name.

Gerald died four years after signing away his name, at exactly the same age as his father: sixty-two. As always, one wonders whether the omnipresent cigarette was partly responsible.

DU MAURIER THE THIRD: *REBECCA*

Tobacco smoke whiffs, atmospherically, over Daphne du Maurier's novel *Rebecca*: most sinisterly from the lips and fingers of the lounge-lizard, Jack Favell – whose seductive techniques are clearly on view when he offers a cigarette to the ineffably virtuous second Mrs de Winter.

Jack was played on screen, in Alfred Hitchcock's 1940 version, by George Sanders – whose smooth cad/toff style was the quintessence of Geraldism. In the cigarette scene, Hitchcock's screenplay closely follows du Maurier's text in which, on their first encounter, after some banter about the dog Jasper, Jack addresses Mrs de Winter, 'in a familiar way':

> Then he pulled out his cigarette case. 'Have one?' he said.
> 'I don't smoke,' I told him.
> 'Don't you really?' He took one himself and lighted it.

She can't quite put her finger on it, but it strikes her as 'rather bad manners'.

At the climax of the action as the de Winters drive home (he having been fraudulently cleared of murder) they find Manderley ablaze. We never know the cause of the fire. Many readers suspect 'Danny' as a last act of revenge and devotion to the woman she pervertedly loved. Those more spiritually inclined will believe it is the ghost of Rebecca: her final self-exorcism. I tend towards the latter explanation – with the additional detail that the spectral lady drops a burning cigarette to get the whole thing going. A du Maurier, of course.

6

Some Curious Literary Records: Best, Worst, and Most

'Ah, but a man's reach should exceed his grasp,
or what's a heaven for?'
Robert Browning (what about Elizabeth Barrett's reach?)

The Worst Novelist Ever

On 26 September 2006 one of the smallest literary festivals ever organised was held in the John Hewitt Bar, Belfast. Small attendance was in order. The festival's mission was to celebrate 'The World's Worst Novelist'.

Amanda McKittrick Ros has always had a loyal band of what, in other circumstances, might be called 'admirers.' She has never, alas, broken into the big time of bad literature to join the world's worst poet, William McGonagall (he, of course, had the inspired support of the world's greatest goon, Spike Milligan). Ros remains a minority taste. Caviare to the general.

Anna Margaret McKittrick was born in 1860, in County Down. 'By birth,' she later proclaimed, 'I am an Irishwoman, though a dash of German blood piebalds my veins.' A clever girl, Miss McKittrick trained as a schoolteacher, and, aged seventeen, married Andy Ross, stationmaster at Larne. For authorial purposes she later knocked an 's' off her married name and borrowed 'Amanda' from the heroines of the gothic fiction she loved. Malicious commentators suggest she wanted to imply association with the aristocratic de Ros family. Or, more likely, she may have wanted to spare Andy's blushes.

Ros's novels and verse were vanity-published; her first with a donation from her husband on their tenth wedding anniversary. Her vanity, it must be said, was more than adequate to her talent. The Ros corpus comprises the novels *Irene Iddesleigh* (1897); *Delina Delaney* (1898); *Donald Dudley* (1900); and *Helen Huddleston* (unfinished at the time of her death, in 1936; as was the similarly promising *The Lusty Lawyer*). There were also two volumes of verse: *Fumes of Formation* (1933) and *Poems of Puncture*

(1913). In later life – ensconced in a house she called 'Iddesleigh' – she was widowed and well-enough propertied from small inheritances to concentrate on her writing.

Generally beneath reviewers' notice, the humorist Barry Pain picked up *Irene Iddesleigh* and was humorous at the author's expense. Amanda struck back by describing the London literateur as a 'cancerous irritant wart'. She composed a celebratory poem on his death, in 1928, rejoicing that there was one less 'pain' in her life. The authoress (as she always termed herself) had the last laugh.

A club of men of letters, including such luminaries of the London literary world as Lord Beveridge, Desmond MacCarthy, and the *Punch*-man F. Anstey, met regularly to compete for the most ludicrous passages from her work they could come up with. In Oxford, the 'Inklings' – donnish fellows (in every sense) such as J.R.R. Tolkien, C.S. Lewis, and Charles Williams, would meet in their favourite pub, the 'Bird and Baby', in the dark days of the 1940s, for readings from the Ros *gesamtwerk* – (or, as the authoress, who preferred French, would have called her collected works, 'my *oeuvre*' despite the dash of German in her veins). The *victor ludorum* was judged to be he who could read longest while keeping the straightest face.

Aldous Huxley also had a Ros-club which met to savour the lady's stylistic flights and felicities. The author of *Brave New World* was, the deluded lady declared 'the only critic who understands my writing'. Her most devoted reader, she fondly believed, was King George V, who had, she claimed, no less than twenty-five copies of her work in his library.

The reverse fandom has continued, cultishly, to the present day. A contemporary website dedicated to the search for the world's worst writers (www.nickpage.co.uk/worstweb) confidently raises Ros's writing arm, winner and still champion, well ahead of her only serious rival for the title, the laureate of cheese, James McIntyre (1827–1906). McIntyre (a Canadian dairy farmer, unsurprisingly) was the author of such works as 'Ode on the Mammoth Cheese'. It opens: 'We have seen thee, queen of cheese, / Lying quietly at your ease', and gets cheesily worse. But not worse enough to rival Ros's sublimities.

Nick Page, host to the above website, hazards that Ros's *Delina Delaney* 'begins with possibly the most baffling opening sentence in *any* literature':

> Have you ever visited that portion of Erin's plot that offers its sympathetic soil for the minute survey and scrutinous examination of those in political power, whose decision has wisely been the means before now of converting the stern and prejudiced, and reaching the hand of slight aid?

My vote would go to the brasher opening sentence of *Irene Iddesleigh*:

> Sympathise with me, Indeed! Ah, No! Cast your sympathy on the chill waves of troubled waters; fling it on the oases of futurity; dash it against the rock of gossip; or better still, allow it to remain within the false and faithless bosom of buried scorn.

It has always seemed to me that the Bulwer-Lytton Fiction Society, who launched their annual 'Dark and Stormy Night' competition for the worst first line in 1982, were wrong to name it after the author of *Paul Clifford*. If there was any justice in the literary world, the name 'Ros' should be on that uncoveted trophy.

Those curious about the authoress are directed to the definitive (and commendably kind) biography, *O Rare Amanda!*, by Jack Loudan (1954).

THE BEST NOVEL(IST) EVER

There is, alas, no clear contender for the 'Shakespeare of Fiction Award' – at least, not in English literature. In Spain, Cervantes would certainly qualify. But *Don Quixote* would probably also win any poll for the greatest work of fiction no one, other than Spaniards, ever reads to the end.

Gallant attempts have been made. Notably in 2007, when in commemoration of 'World Book Day', two thousand British bibliophiles were polled as to what was the 'most essential' book in their language. Novels swept the board. The following were the top ten (with percentages):

1. *Pride and Prejudice* (20%)
2. *The Lord of the Rings* (17%)
3. *Jane Eyre* (14%)
4. The Harry Potter series (12%)
5. *To Kill a Mockingbird* (9.5%)
6. The Bible (9%)
7. *Wuthering Heights* (8.5%)
8. *Nineteen Eighty-Four* (6%)
8. 'His Dark Materials' (6%)
10. *Great Expectations* (5%)

Spot the non-fiction work. Or, perhaps not. What with the frenzied debates about Creationism in the US, and the Dawkins-led assault on Holy Writ in the UK, the 'Greatest Story Ever Told' (as Hollywood called it) might conceivably qualify with all the lesser stories ever told for the fiction shelf in any progressive bookstore, particularly an outlet catering to younger patrons. The

Bible came in the top four with the over-sixties but was ranked at nineteen with the under-eighteens. At least God beat the atheistic Philip Pullman in the greatness stakes. And He's always been in it for the long game; the final judgement, as you might say. And when those four trumpets blast, and the dead rise, which of us would like to look Him in the eye and say Hogwarts was more 'essential'?

There are other measures for the greatness award. The most studied novel in US high schools is, it is curious to discover, *The Great Gatsby*. In Taiwan, the most studied English text is *Jane Eyre* but in South Korea apparently *Wuthering Heights* (a Queen's Award for Export to Haworth). The novel which has been longest in continuous print in the English-speaking world, racking up tens of millions of sales over the centuries, is *The Pilgrim's Progress*. *Pride and Prejudice*'s pride of place was confirmed by a 2006 poll among librarians who confirmed that Miss Austen's novel had the nation's 'favourite happy ending' (everyone knows the first – 'truth universally acknowledged' – sentence; but how many of us can, without peeking, remember the novel's curtain line? Or that rather ominous remark dropped by Elizabeth that she first fell in love with Darcy on seeing Pemberley?)

The novels which, in adaptation, have attracted the largest number of English eyeballs are Andrew Davies's TV adaptation of *Middlemarch* (1994) and his later adaptation of Trollope's *The Way We Live Now* (2001). Both came in at 7 million-plus viewers. Worldwide gross receipts for the 2005 film of *Pride and Prejudice* (at the time of writing), are $121,147,947. At an average ten dollars a cinema seat (and ignoring DVD, and TV audiences) one can hazard some 12 million fans of Keira Knightley's delectable Elizabeth Bennett.

The novel, one may say, still awaits its Shakespeare. But the audiences get larger all the time.

'Greatest Story Ever Told' Novels

Religious bestsellers (i.e., those that centrally feature Christ, or his apostles) have always figured intermittently on the American bestseller list, but never on the British. For example:

Ben Hur (1880), Lew Wallace
Quo Vadis (1896), Henryk Sienkiewicz
In His Steps (1897), Charles M. Sheldon
The Big Fisherman (1942), Lloyd C. Douglas
The Robe (1943), Lloyd C. Douglas
Kingdom Come (2007), Tim LaHaye and Jerry B. Jenkins

These chiliastic resurgences seem to mean something, but it is hard to say what – other than religion sells in the US.

MY PEN IS QUICK

Fast-order fiction was Mickey Spillane's speciality. *I, the Jury*, his first Mike Hammer novel, was tossed off in nine days. It went on to sell 7 million copies in three years. When the car containing his manuscript of *The Body Lovers* was stolen, Spillane claimed only to be concerned about the loss of his wheels: 'the missing manuscript just means another three days' work'. No publisher ever had to wait for Mr Spillane.

There have been other quick-on-the-draw pens. Alexandre Dumas wagered a hundred louis (a sizeable sum in 1845) that he could write the first volume of his next three-decker, *Le Chevalier de Maison Rouge*, in three days. Fuelled by copious draughts of coffee (a substance with which, scholars tell us, Dumas's manuscripts are liberally spattered) he pulled the feat off, writing 34,000 words with six hours to spare. There was 'scarcely an erasure', but some coffee spatter. Whether, like Spillane, he could have done it twice in a week, if some rogue stole his horse and carriage, is something else.

Jack Kerouac favoured a higher-octane fuel. He would drop in his coffee Benzedrine pellets taken from nasal inhalants. 'One lump or two?' meant something quite different for Jack. In 1941, with a free ream of yellow paper and a rented Underwood – the first machine he laid fingers on – Kerouac claimed to have dashed off 'something like two hundred short stories in about eight weeks'.

None of this rapid-fire fiction proved publishable. But, as Kerouac liked to say, 'walking on water wasn't built in a day'. Fame came to the King of the Beats in 1957, with *On the Road*. Another of his grandiloquent critical mottos was 'You're a Genius all the time', which may have been true for him, although critical respect for his genius melted away when he failed to follow up with anything as good as *On the Road*. It was less the Benzedrine than the booze, biography suggests.

Alcohol rarely accelerates genius, although sometimes it can. Stephen King, for example, recalls writing his pseudonymised 'Bachman' book, *The Running Man*, in three days, at a period when, as he elsewhere recalls, his fuel was a nightly case of Budweiser. Running Man, Rushing Author.

Inspired by such feats of literary athleticism, Pulp Press International, based in Vancouver, launched its 'Three-Day Novel Contest', in 1978. The event has been held, more or less annually, by various sponsoring bodies over the last thirty years.[*]

---

[*] For those who are curious, a list of the thirty-three winners since 1979 can be found on wikipedia and the entry rules, for those with three days to spare, and a couple of Benzedrine pellets, or whatever, at http://www.3daynovel.com.

No masterpieces of *The Body Lovers* class are recorded as emerging.

SLOW COACH

If Spillane holds a speed record for fiction, many would propose Harold Brodkey (1930–96) as the slowest of literary coaches. He started fast enough, exploding on the literary scene with a clutch of short stories for the *New Yorker*, in the very early 1950s. William Shawn's magazine was then a red-carpet to literary fame. The world was at Harold Brodkey's feet. But the feet never moved. Thereafter his career was silence and rumour.

It was put about that Brodkey was embarked on a gigantic work. Possibly the greatest Great American Novel ever. A work which would make *Moby Dick* look like a newly spawned minnow. Six thousand pages was mentioned. He had, it was further intimated, been working on this novel since childhood. It would be called *A Party of Animals*. The title gave nothing away.

A provisional manuscript (some 5,000 pages, it was said) had been lodged with Brodkey's publisher, Farrar Straus & Giroux, 'in a form so that if something happens to me, someone can deal with it'. Indeed something did happen to him. Brodkey contracted HIV in the 1970s, as he claimed. If so, the symptoms were (like his publishing output) abnormally slow. They did not appear for fifteen years. He was not, Brodkey insisted, gay; but, like many writers, experimental by nature. And unluckier than most.

His readers had a long, forty-year, wait and an anticlimactic one. In 1991 there finally appeared the work which the world had been on tenterhooks to see. It was entitled *The Runaway Soul* and ran to a mere 853 printed pages. Brodkey announced that it was only the first instalment of *A Party of Animals*. He was sixty-one. Methuselah couldn't have finished the work at this rate.

He died in January 1996 of Aids within the same forty-eight hours, curiously, as Joseph Brodsky – the Nobel Prize-winning writer with whom, to Brodkey's irritation he was perennially confused during life; and now, dammit, in death.

In his last two years Brodkey penned a poignant account of his end, *This Wild Darkness: The Story of My Death*. An *ars moriendi* (a venerable but obsolete genre) it traces his painful journey to the dying of the light. In it, he seems, at times, to mount a defence of the snail-like pace of his work. Published a few months after his death, he cannot quite be said to have to beaten the undertaker in the race to the finishing line, but he gallantly finished the course. His great novel didn't.

HARDEST WORKING

Many candidates propose themselves for the award of 'hardest-working novelist'. One might, perhaps, call it the 'Trollope memorial prize' in memory of literature's most self-advertisingly Stakhanovite of the pen (Alexey Stakhanov was the Soviet Union's most famous miner and a 'Hero of Socialist Labour'. He set an all-time record by mining 227 tons of coal in a single shift.) If writing fiction were a clan activity, the Trollope family between them would sweep the board. Anthony's mother, the indomitable Mrs Fanny Trollope, his sister Cecilia, his brother Thomas, and his sister-in-law Frances can claim 114 titles between them. Beats 227 tons of coal any day.

My candidate, though, would be Mrs Oliphant, author of some ninety-five big Victorian novels. Widowed in her twenties, with two young children to support, Mrs Oliphant actually wore a hole in her finger writing fiction.

Runner-up, in the Victorian stakes, would be L[illie] T[oulmin] Meade, a Victorian pioneer writer of fiction for girls, who has no less than 251 full-length works deposited in the British Library – all, alas, as unknown to posterity as the author herself. This mother of chick-lit died, worn out, at sixty.

Stakhanovite heroes of the twentieth-century pen would be headed by John Creasey (creator of the 'Toff'), whose tally of 564 (some counts put it higher) exceeds even that of Simenon (500), who proudly claimed to have slept with twenty times as many women of the night – putting him in contention for two world titles.

Genre, unsurprisingly, dominates the big-score league. The list would include 'king of the thrillers', Edgar Wallace. The author of some 175 novels (and much else), Wallace's appeal in his heyday extended well beyond that of the brand-loyal fan. It was claimed (perhaps hyperbolically) that in the 1920s a quarter of all the books read in England were by him, and that his sales were second only to those of the Bible (another score for the deity to settle on Judgement Day). He died midway through collaborating on the screenplay for the 1934 movie, *King Kong* – ironically the only one of his works which has really lasted in popular memory: although few attach his name to it.

Not for Wallace any holes in the writing finger. He composed his works on a dictaphone, sustained by gallons of sweet, weak tea, in a glass-walled office.

Hardest Reading

How hard or easy it is depends, of course, on the reader. But prime candidates for the SAS version of a literary obstacle course might include:

Sordello: as Robert Browning said, when he wrote it, only he and God knew what it meant. Twenty years later, only God.

Finnegans Wake: Joyce took a quarter of a lifetime to write it, and instructed that it would need a lifetime to read it. Methuselah, some say, would not make it.

A Void (La Disparition): Georges Perec undertook to write this 300-page 'thriller' without once using the letter 'e'. Well done Gorgs Prc.

Gadsby: an earlier novel that gets by without the letter 'e' by Ernest Vincent Wright. Few have heard of it and those that have think it's by Scott Fitzgerald.

Time's Arrow: a novel narrated backwards by Amis Martin.

Any poetry by John Ashbery, Ron Silliman, or Basil Bunting.

Gravity's Rainbow: by Thomas Pynchon. The dragon at the gate of post-modernism.

As a teacher, I once offered a course called 'impossible literature' featuring some of the above texts. It attracts a difficult kind of student, I discover.

THE MOST ARDUOUS

If there were a special Olympics for writing, it would be a run-off between Larry Eigner and Christy Brown, the two most indomitably disabled-but-gifted authors in the annals of literature.

Eigner, a poet, suffered forceps injury during birth which led to life-long cerebral palsy. He could only compose his poems by tap-typing with his right index finger – rather like an old-fashioned telegraph operator, but without the dexterity that would enable him to do it at more than a stroke every few seconds. Writing for him was what speaking was for the older Stephen Hawking.

None the less, Eigner published some forty books, and hundreds of other pieces. As Darren Wershler-Henry points out, in his 'fragmented history of typewriting', Eigner's laboriously digital mode of production had a formative effect on his style. For him, as for William Carlos Williams, a poem was 'a machine made of words'. But for him, the words were less written, than hewn. As he said: 'letters get crowded just from my attempt to save time, i.e., to cover less space, avoid putting another sheet in the typewriter for a few more words'.

A representative quotation from Eigner's poem entitled '#31' in the collection entitled *The* illustrates the point:

> up and
> down
> nothing
> sound ends

Writing as he did, Eigner was a major influence on the younger L=A=N=G=U=A=G=E school of poets, of whom the leader is the wonderfully named Ron Silliman. The 'physicality' of Eigner's technique feeds through, as a kind of lyric pain, into the words on the page. To adapt Truman Capote's insult about Jack Kerouac into praise: 'that's not writing: that's typing'. Great typing.

Like Eigner, Christy Brown was afflicted with cerebral palsy: congenital, in his case, and resulting in virtually total paralysis. Even were he not so cruelly disabled, Brown had the cards stacked against him as a budding author. Born in 1932, at the height of the world slump, the son of an Irish bricklayer, Christy was one of twenty-two children (seventeen survived). No silver spoons in the Brown household.

In his childhood Christy was presumed to be mentally defective until, aged five, he picked up a piece of chalk with his left foot, and began desperately attempting to scrawl the letter 'A' with it. There was, the family realised, somebody inside that ruined body, trying to get out.

His mother, who had always 'believed' in him, taught the boy to read and write. Mrs Brown was aided by a local doctor and specialist in cerebral palsy, Bob Collis. Over the years, with intensive care, Brown gained basic language skills and sufficient physical mobility to single-finger, or single toe-type. 'My education', he writes:

> was practically nil. The first and only bit of education I ever had was learning the alphabet from mother at the age of five. I had gone on from there the best way I could on my own, teaching myself to read books – mostly Dickens! – to learn all I could from them.

Like Eigner again, the keyboard was Brown's gateway to authorship. His autobiography, *My Left Foot*, took him ten years. It was published in 1954, and became a bestseller, as did the spun-off novel, *Down all the Days* (1970). The film starring Daniel Day-Lewis was released in 1987 to wide acclaim. Before his death, in 1981, Brown had established himself as a poet and artist – and, as Collis put it, 'proof of the amazing power of the spirit of man to overcome the impossible.'

A writer faced with obstacles even more impossible than Brown – with his left foot – was the paralysed Jean-Dominique Bauby, who dictated his post-stroke memoir, *Le Scaphandre et le Papillon* (*The Diving Bell and the Butterfly*) with an alphabetic code, involving 200,000 blinks of his left eyelid, the one functioning part of his body.

CHALK, PEN, OR TYPEWRITER?

In late June 2007, Brown's widow, Mary, put up for auction in Dublin the Olympia Splendid 99 typewriter on which, the sales catalogue asserted, the author had tapped out *My Left Foot*.

Brown's sister, Ann, contradicted the statement, saying that he wrote the autobiography, as the title indicated, with a pencil grasped in his foot and only later mastered the typewriter.

The machine (expected to draw a price as high as €15,000) was withdrawn from sale by the auctioneers, James Adam and Sons, until the issue was settled.

LITTLE WRITING

In my early career, I worked on writers' manuscripts. Mainly it was nineteenth-century fiction. The worst handwriting, by far, was Bulwer-Lytton's: or, to overload this sentence with his full name (and title): 'Edward George Earle Lytton Bulwer-Lytton, Bart.' That opening line to *Paul Clifford* ('It was a dark and stormy night') which has inspired such mirth and an annual competition for the worst opening line of the year could as well, to my eye, have been 'It were a dirgle and streamy niggle'.

Some years into my academic career I was asked by a descendant of the Bulwer-Lyttons if I might be interested in doing the 'life'. The prospect of wading through the tangled barbed wire of Bulwerian script was too much. I left the task to braver and younger eyes than mine.

Trollope and Scott were both, in their youth, trained scriveners and it shows in their eminently legible handwriting. Trollope recalls the embarrassment of his recruitment as a clerk in the Post Office:

> I was asked to copy some lines from *The Times* newspaper with an old quill pen, and at once made a series of blots and false spellings.

'That won't do,' he was politely told. Young Anthony got the message and quickly acquired the necessary penmanship – along with the clerk's fluency, and page-by-page metronome rhythm. Hence the famous Trollopian 'method' and the clerical measurements he puts at the head of his manuscripts. For example, that for the greatest of his novels, *The Way We Live Now*:

Carbury Novel. 20 Numbers. 64 Pages each Number. 260 Words
each Page. 40 Pages a Week. To be completed in 32 Weeks.

This is Trollope the Clerk writing, not the Chronicler of
Barsetshire.

Young Walter Scott began his working life as a copy-clerk in his
father, Walter Scott Sr's, Edinburgh law office. At his desk in that
office young Walter was not merely a scrivener: he was the champion scrivener. On one occasion, he copied 120 pages in a single
day, earning a phenomenal 30 shillings. As a relic of his appren-
ticeship in the 'old shop' (as he called it) Scott, to the end of his
career, retained the reflexive clerical habit of ending the quarto
page of his fiction with a curly scroll down from the last line of
script to the bottom margin, so that nothing could be illicitly
inserted.

The most beautiful, and legible, handwriting in nineteenth-
century fiction is Thackeray's. The novelist had two composi-
tional styles: slanted copperplate and upright. He varied the
scripts according to mood: both his, and the narrative context.
Both styles are found, interestingly varied, in the surviving MS
of *Vanity Fair*.

Thackeray was also a virtuoso of miniature script. One of his
party tricks was to inscribe the Lord's Prayer on the back of a
penny-black postage stamp or – even more demandingly – a dry
cherry pip.

The Nobel Prize-winning theoretical physicist, Richard Feynman
– whose research dealt with particles so small that no human eye
will ever see them – was fascinated by nano-technology. On 29
December 1959, he gave what would become a famous after-dinner
talk to the American Physical Society. It was entitled 'Plenty of

Room at the Bottom' and ruminated on the huge future of minia-turisation. 'They tell me,' said Feynman, 'about electric motors that are the size of the nail on your small finger':

> And there is a device on the market, they tell me, by which you can write the Lord's Prayer on the head of a pin. But that's nothing; that's the most primitive, halting step in the direction I intend to discuss. It is a staggeringly small world that is below. In the year 2000, when they look back at this age, they will wonder why it was not until the year 1960 that anybody began seriously to move in this direction. Why cannot we write the entire twenty-four volumes of the *Encyclopaedia Britannica* on the head of a pin?

The following year, Feynman offered a prize for anyone able to pull off that ultraminiature writing feat. This, recall, was 1960: barely beyond the cherry-pip era.

It was not until 1985 that a graduate student at Stanford, Tom Newman, won Feynman's prize. He did not do the whole *Britannica*, but demonstrated the feasibility by inscribing the first page of Dickens's *A Tale of Two Cities* ('it was the best of times, it was the worst of times', etc.) at 1/25,000th its size on a pinhead. It was the smallest of times. And, as Feynman predicted, it is getting smaller all the time.

As Feynman's biographers, John and Mary Gribbin, record:

> The main problem Newman had before he could claim the prize was finding the text (using an electron microscope) after he had written it – the head of a pin was a huge empty space compared with the page of text inscribed on it.

POSTSCRIPT: Thackeray's feat, writing the Lord's Prayer on the back of a penny black is, so to speak, dwarfed by the achievement of Ernest L. Blystone, who in the 1930s wrote the Lord's Prayer on a hair and was said to be able to write it 101 times inside 'a circle the size of a dime'.

Writing Long

The longest novel in the literary canon is generally held to be Samuel Richardson's *Clarissa* which in its third expanded (!) edition comes in at around a million words. Very helpfully the novelist offers chapter synopses in which encapsulated form *Clarissa* also qualifies as one of the shorter narratives in the language.

When Mrs Humphry Ward sent the manuscript of *Robert Elsmere* to the publisher in 1881, it was some 750,000 words – which would have put it up there with the big ones.

George Smith, alas, demurred. He did not want for the House of Smith, Elder & Co. the glory of publishing the baggiest 'baggy monster' (Henry James's term) of the century. The editorial shears were taken to Mrs Ward's magnum opus. Too magnum by half. Oddly, the reading world has never called for an uncut *Robert Elsmere*, as it has with Stephen King's *The Stand* which, in its uncut form, comes in at 464,216 words. Enough for even the most loyal fan.

Novels like *The Stand* are not easy for those without considerable upper body strength – demanding a kind of 'snatch and press' technique if one is to hoist them into a readable position. As the reviewer said of James Michener's docunovel, *Texas* (a puny 350,000 or so words), 'don't drop it on your foot' (and, he added, for strangers to the author, a second piece of advice: 'don't read it'). Less blockbuster than toebuster.

The first blockbuster (i.e., extravagantly long novel) to head the American bestseller list was Hervey Allen's *Anthony Adverse*, published in 1933. At 1,200 pages, comprising some 400,000 words, and costing a whopping (for then) $3, the publishers, Farrar and Rinehart, advertised Allen's eighteenth-century tale of buccaneering and adventure on the high seas as 'three books for the price of one' and 'the longest novel ever published'. It was both block and blockbuster. Boosted as a Book of the Month Club title, and by an Oscar-winning 1936 film adaptation, *Anthony Adverse* topped the American bestseller list for two years. A notable innovation was the novel's sexual explicitness, with scenes set in brothels and direct reference to 'erections' and 'orgasms' (an aspect of the novel prudently excised for the mass-movie audience). The implication was that young, impressionable readers were not drawn to really big books.

In the UK in the twentieth century, Vikram Seth's *A Suitable Boy* weighed in at 591,554 words, and is plausibly claimed to be 'the longest single-volume novel ever to be published in English'. Seth discovered, unsurprisingly, that 'publishers aren't intrinsically fond of long novels', for the good reason that modern readers aren't intrinsically fond of them. He offered to cut a finger off for every 10,000 words over the hundred that his next novel went and has since kept within conventional bounds.

The sequence, or saga, novels of Anthony Trollope and Anthony Powell, in which characters and situations are carried over, creating massively overarching narratives, dwarf any single work. The six novels which make up Trollope's 'Palliser' series come in at around 2 million words, and Anthony Powell's 'Dance to the Music of Time' series is as long, if not longer.

The longest play in the repertoire of the English stage is Shaw's 'metabiological pentateuch' *Back to Methuselah*, closely followed by his Wagnerian *Man and Superman*. Eugene O'Neill's *Strange Interlude* – a play which multiplies its performance time by interjecting the characters' thought processes – runs to four hours. It won a Pulitzer in 1928. One wonders how the notorious 'Broadway bladder' coped.

WRITING SHORT

The shortest play of any critical standing is Samuel Beckett's minimalist masterpiece, *Breath*. One could cite it in its entirety, did copyright allow. But, in synopsis, this is the whole action (if that's the right word). The stage curtain parts to illumine ('faintly') some rubbish. This shot is held for five seconds. There is a 'faint brief' cry, the sound of breathing-in ('inspiration') and a bit more light (Beckett's stage direction instructs on how much). This climaxes in ten seconds. The light then fades and the silence creeps back over the next five seconds, accompanied by the sound of breathing out ('expiration'). The curtain falls and it's back home. God help any latecomers. You could miss the play by unwrapping your first chocolate. It is, of course, the human narrative reduced to 'a man is born, lives, and dies (expires)'.

Short novels take one into 'how long is a piece of string' territory. But there is an annual quarrel on the subject, provoked by the Man Booker Prize. The rules clearly state that the prize shall be awarded to the author of the 'best, eligible, full-length novel of the year in the opinion of the judges'. That awkwardly inserted criterion, 'full-length', forestalls any Beckettian nonsense.

In 2007, one of the short-listed favourites was Ian McEwan's *On Chesil Beach*. Well reviewed, and bestselling, it was the bookies' odds-on favourite in the run-up to the gala evening in October, when the winner is announced. But was it, argument raged, 'full-length'? At 38,000 words was it not a 'novella'?

'That's their problem, not mine, I think,' McEwan blandly commented. After the usual sagacious consideration, the judges awarded the prize to the indubitably full-length work *The Gathering* by Anne Enright. Close on three *Chesil Beach*es, if one wants to measure that way. 'Forget the width, feel the quality', McEwan's supporters say.

The shortest novel ever written is often attributed to Ernest Hemingway, who came up with: 'For sale: One pair of baby shoes. Never worn.' He didn't copyright it, which means one may quote the work in its entirety. Hemingway's *The Old Man and the Sea* remains the shortest novel ever to win the Pulitzer Prize.

An Armful of Toebusters

In Search of Lost Time, Marcel Proust, *Guinness Book of Records* holder, with an estimated 3 million words

Atlas Shrugged, Ayn Rand, 645,000 words

War and Peace, Leo Tolstoy, 560,000 words

Infinite Jest, David Foster Wallace, 479,198 words

The Count of Monte Cristo, Alexandre Dumas, 464, 234 words.

Thanks for these number-counts to wikipedia and amazon consultant, 'cervantes625'. Howard S. Berg – who is credited in the *Guinness Book of Records* with a reading speed of 25,000 words a minute could polish off all of the above in well under three finger-spraining, eye-straining hours.

THE SHORTEST POEM

The poet Allen Ginsberg, web-legend has it, died not with his trademark howl, but a chirpy 'toodle-oo' to those he left behind. If so, it was a quaint farewell from the laureate of the Beats: he who had seen the best minds of his generation destroyed by madness, starving hysterical naked, dragging themselves through the negro streets at dawn looking for an angry fix. Was he, one wonders, reading P.G. Wodehouse to ease his last hours on earth?

Ginsberg's last words (word?) were not poetry – but they were so transmuted soon after. The companion of his most anarchic Beat years (his Jeeves, one might say) was Gregory Corso – an elegant, but less brilliant, luminary in that doomed band of creative freaksters. When his mentor died, in 1997, Corso attended the memorial service for which he recited to the other mourners what he described as a one-word poem: 'Toodle-oo'.

Corso may well be the author of the shortest original poem in the English language, although Dylan Thomas also has a claim to the title. On seeing a young woman with magnificent frontage (tight sweaters over D-cup busts were wildly exciting to males in the early 1950s) Thomas declared he would, on the spot, write the shortest, and most beautiful poem ever to pass human lips. He then wolf-whistled and leered, lecherously. And hopefully. The poem has to be whistled with a Welsh accent for its full effect. The above story was told to me by Philip Larkin, although he did not – as one can see – include Thomas's whistle-work in his *Oxford Book of Twentieth-Century English Verse* (controversial as that compilation was).

'Toodle-oo' is more honk than whistle. One convincing etymology traces it to the raucous, goose-like, warning call rubber-bulb klaxons made on Edwardian motor cars – like Mr Toad's 'poop-poop!' – as they sped on their way (that warning noise, incidentally, mutates into the analogous farewell 'pip pip!'). Another folk etymology suggests that 'toodle-oo' derives from the French *'toute à l'heure'* (see you soon!) as distorted by the philistine English ear and tongue.

The last derivation seems as likely as any. The term was given great currency by the music hall song, popular in World War I, 'Goodbye-ee!', sung by soldiers on their way to France, reassuring those left behind to keep the home fires burning:

> Goodbye-ee! Goodbye-ee!
> Wipe a tear, baby dear, from your eye-ee.
> Though it's hard to part, I know,
> I'll be tickled to death to go.
> Don't cry-ee! Don't sigh-ee!
> There's a silver lining in the sky-ee.
> Bon soir old thing! Cheerio, chin-chin!
> Nah-poo! Toodle-oo! Goodbye-ee!

And just what does Nah-poo mean?

As a deflationary postscript Ginsberg's 'toodle-oo!' – although universally vouched for by web know-alls – is, alas, apocryphal. Most famous last words are. According to Graham Caveney's *Screaming with Joy: the Life of Allen Ginsberg* (1999) the poet died in 1997 from cancer of the liver and his last word was 'a weak "aah!"' Short, indeed, but no poem there.

Shortened Poem, Never-ending Poem

One of the more drastically shortened poems in the canon is the fourth section of T.S. Eliot's *The Waste Land*, which '*il miglior fabbro*', Ezra Pound, whittled down from many many stanzas to ten elliptical lines. The shortest narrative poem in the English language, however, is generally taken to be 'Fleas':

Adam
Had'em

(Author unknown and wholly un-canonical).

The longest poem was unrolled, inscribed on cloth, by the French public notary and poet, Patrick Huet, along a kilometre of the Champier car racetrack, in August 2006. More fun to drive it than read it, one imagines. Seven thousand stanzas long (where is *il miglior fabbro* when you need him?) it is called *Pieces of Hope to the Echo of the World*. If those are the pieces, one hopes never to see the the whole.

THE MOST PRODUCTIVE HOLIDAY IN ENGLISH LITERATURE

Asked what was the most productive summer holiday in literary history, one would have to opt for that which took place in July

1816 at Lake Geneva. Byron, Mary Shelley, Percy Shelley and Dr John Polidori were the vacationers. The outcome of that momentous holiday forms the subject of Benjamin Markovits's 2007 novel, *Imposture*. The weather was utterly 'miserable' – so much so that none of the company could leave the villa they had taken, overlooking the lake. As Markovits records:

> To relieve the boredom they began to recite ghost stories to each other, and it was only a matter of time, among so many writers, before they attempted their own.

Mary Shelley, still a teenager, came up with *Frankenstein,* published in 1818. Polidori (possibly with the assistance of Byron, and certainly inspired in his depiction of evil incarnate by the mad, bad, lord) came up with *The Vampyre*, published in 1819. Percy's effort was not so wonderful.

Thus were two of the richest franchises in fiction created: neither (to Hollywood's eternal gratitude) trademarked.

What if the sun had been shining brilliantly, as it should have been at that season of the year? Would there be blank spaces where all the Frankenstein and Dracula knock-offs, homages, and rip offs now lodge on our shelves? What would Anne Rice have done without a century and a half's vampirology to draw on, all stemming from Polidori's parlour entertainment?

There is, curiously, an explanation as to why the weather was so miserable and perversely inspirational. In the scientific journal *Nature* in July 1997, Euan Nisbet, a member of the geology department at Royal Holloway College, London, analysed data to be found in *The Climate of London*, by Luke Howard, published in 1833. It is, one is told, 'one of the founding texts of British meteorology'.

As Howard records, 1816 was 'the year without a summer',

after the eruption of the Tambora volcano. 1816 is also known as the 'poverty' year. Crops failed. There was famine and violence. Switzerland was particularly badly affected.

Those reading *Frankenstein*, Bram Stoker's *Dracula*, and *Imposture* may well think that it's an ill wind (or volcano) that blows no good. The rain that made summer 2007 so record-breakingly wretched in the UK may, by way of compensation, bring forth a bumper crop of fiction. Man Booker judges stand by.

Youngest and Oldest Novelists

The youngest writer to have won a place in the pantheon of Great English Literature is Daisy Ashford, who wrote *The Young Visiters, or, Mister Salteena's Plan* (initially for the admiration of her father), aged nine. It was introduced to the world in 1919, by J.M. Barrie (the creator of Peter Pan, appropriately enough) and has been agelessly delighting readers ever since. The oldest novelist to have broken into bestselling print is a contemporary of young Miss Ashford's, William de Morgan, a famous ceramicist and disciple of William Morris. In his sixties de Morgan fell into depression and was advised to write some fiction, by way of therapy. The result was *Joseph Vance* (1906), a first novel published when its author was a mere sixty-seven. It was a huge bestseller, and six other novels followed. The therapy was evidently literary Prozac.

Most Misquoted

It was one of the great bloopers of history. What Neil Armstrong meant to say was 'That's one small step for *a* man; one giant leap for mankind.' What the listening millions on earth heard was: 'That's one small step for man; one giant leap for mankind.'

Armstrong blew the first words ever said by man on extra-terrestrial soil. All that NASA preparation – and they forgot the voice coach. If ever Lynne Truss wanted an example for the importance of the little bits of speech – that's it. Written in the stars.

As a result of Armstrong's mis-speak, for the best part of four decades humanity's inaugural extraterrestrial utterance has been as nonsensical as Monty Python's 'Blessed are the cheesemakers' (on notable cheesemakers, by the way, see p. 95).

Hi-tech (the highest ever) projected Armstrong off earth. Hi-tech eventually, after decades of sniggering, saved Armstrong from the shame of perpetrating the first extraterrestrial misquote. A blooper in the same category as Columbus thinking he'd landed in East Indies – thus lumbering Native Americans with the misleading name which they are, to this day, trying to shake off.

In 2006 cutting-edge audio-technology discovered that Armstrong did, in point of fact, insert the indefinite article but so rapidly that it got lost in the white noise of radio transmission travelling, cracklingly, 220,000 miles across the ether.

Glad as one was to have the record put straight, the sad fact is that, when it comes to (mis)quotes, we often stubbornly prefer the fabrication, or the distortion, over the real thing. As the Italians

Great Books, Big Blunders

There are numerous candidates for the biggest blunder award, from Shakespeare's assumption that Bohemia has a coastline, through Walter Scott having the sun set in the east (in *The Antiquary*) to Piggy's eye-glasses being used to make fire in *Lord of the Flies*. But among the most persistent, and most loved, is found in the film of *The Third Man*, scripted by Graham Greene. The movie is most famous for two things Greene had nothing to do with – Anton Karas's haunting zither, and the villain, Harry Lime's, speech:

> Like the fella says, in Italy for thirty years under the Borgias they had warfare, terror, murder, and bloodshed, but they produced Michelangelo, Leonardo da Vinci, and the Renaissance. In Switzerland they had brotherly love – they had 500 years of democracy and peace, and what did that produce? *The cuckoo clock.*

The speech was actually the composition of Orson Welles, who played Lime. It's great writing, but lousy horology. The cuckoo clock was invented in the mid-eighteenth century in southern Germany: the period which gave the world Goethe, Kant, Schiller, Beethoven and Hegel – and the region which gave the world Adolf Hitler's Nazi party.

say '*se non è vero, è ben trovato*'. Translation: it may not be true, but, goddammit, I like it.

Which of the following these-you-have-loved is *ben trovato*, and which *vero*?

1: Congreve: 'Hell hath no fury like a woman scorned'.
2: Sherlock Holmes: 'the game's afoot!'
3: Edgar Rice Burroughs's Tarzan: 'Me Tarzan, You Jane'.
4: Holmes (again): 'Elementary, my dear Watson'.
5: Hamlet: 'Alas, poor Yorick, I knew him well'.
6: Coleridge: 'Water, water everywhere, and not a drop to drink'.
7: Dante: 'Abandon hope, all ye who enter here'.

All are, more or less, misquotes.

The same technology which belatedly excavated that missing syllable from the blurry depths of Neil Armstrong's quote, could, with no trouble at all, insert it audibly into the acoustic record. Should we do it?

I think not; any more than lovers of Robert Louis Stevenson's work would want the misquotation on his gravestone in Samoa chiselled out. It's from his own poem, 'Requiem'. Whoever did the engraving (probably hurriedly, since it was the tropics and bodies decay fast) inserted an unauthorised 'the' before 'sea' in the lines:

> Home is the sailor, home from sea,
> And the hunter home from the hill.

One can see why. 'From sea' is awkward and the tongue stumbles. But if it's there, in stone to boot, leave it. It's human error.

The great painters of the Renaissance, legend has it, would insert mistakes into their designs, as an act of humility. There's something reassuringly human in the fact that 'mankind' can project itself into the heavens, but the guy carrying the flag can't get his lines quite right. Any more than the guy with the chisel.

7
Literary Crimewatch (and Gunplay)

'Foul deeds will rise.' *Hamlet*

Rape and the Ethical Classroom

When the novelist and great thinker Arthur Koestler died (Roman style: by his own hand) he left his million-pound estate to set up a professorial chair in parapsychology at some eminent British university. Oxford, Cambridge, and London were, however, uninterested – regarding what Koestler posthumously proposed as either junk science or joke science; one might as well set up a department of spiritualism and appoint a professor of table-rapping ('Can you hear me, Arthur? One knock, yes.').

Edinburgh, defying obloquy, accepted the Koestlerian gift horse, and duly endowed the chair. It remains the only such in the country. In honour of the donor, a bronze bust of Koestler was commissioned and put on public display. Doubtless undergraduates in the university's English department, after regarding it, read the author's classic novel, *Darkness at Noon* (a principal source for Orwell's *Nineteen Eighty-Four*) with renewed interest.

The bust, however, turned out to be a second source of embarrassment ten years later when David Cesarani published his unauthorised biography of Koestler, *The Homeless Mind* (1998). In it, he indicted Koestler as a covert, serial, and horribly brutal rapist. One victim, Jill Craigie (wife of the statesman, Michael Foot), was particularly convincing in her accusations. Koestler, as one of his other female contemporaries told me, was universally regarded, in rest-room gossip, as NSIT ('Not Safe in Taxis'). But what Cesarani alleged went further. The man, as he portrayed him, was not safe anywhere that didn't have bars on the window and darkness at noon.

Authorial Felonies

Norman Mailer: attempted uxoricide (see p. 135)

Lord Byron: incest (with his half-sister, Augusta) and pederastic sodomy with adolescent boys. Neither cramped his style as a Don Juan, or as the exiled writer of *Don Juan*.

Joe Orton: library-book mutilation, for which the playwright and his partner, Kenneth Halliwell, were sentenced to six months in prison, in 1962 (the books now reside, pricelessly, in Islington Library's treasure room). Halliwell, the unliterary one of the two, later battered Orton to death.

Oscar Wilde: sentenced to two years' hard labour in 1895 for 'acts of gross indecency with other male persons' (there would have been no such offence before 1885, or after 1967).

Shakespeare: poaching deer in Charlecote Park. Much disputed. Since sixteenth-century punishments ranged from branding through castration to beheading a successful prosecution might have had serious consequences for English literature.

After the publication of Cesarani's book, and much gleeful publicity in the papers, Koestler's bust at Edinburgh University was removed into protective storage to avoid attacks from enraged students – feminists, principally, who threatened to take hammer and chisel (gelding shears being no longer efficacious) to the offending memorial, as their co-ideologues routinely did to the final

John Bunyan: imprisoned for twelve years for preaching without a licence. In was in the Bedford Gaol that he wrote *The Pilgrim's Progress*. Bunyan is the longest-serving literary jailbird recorded in *The Oxford Companion to English Literature*.

Daniel Defoe: pilloried and briefly imprisoned in 1703 for a pamphlet arguing for the right to non-conformity (he is the only famous author to have stood, literally, in the stocks and been pelted by his critics).

Sir Thomas Wyatt: imprisoned for treason in 1542. It was during an earlier incarceration in the Tower of London that Wyatt (probably) wrote his most famous poem, 'They flee from me, that sometime did me seek'.

One searches in vain for equivalent women malefactors. None, for example, is listed in the Oxford *Companion* mentioned above. Authorial crime (other than the flagrant breaking of contractual delivery dates) is, it would seem, like the writing of epics (see p. 150) a male preserve.

word on the gravestone of Sylvia Plath *Hughes*, at Heptonstall in Yorkshire.

Oddly, however, two other rapists (or suspected rapists) had a free pass from the Edinburgh militants. In the English department then, and to this day, every junior honours student is obliged to study, in detail, the works of Chaucer. No protests (other than the familiar complaints about irrelevantly old literature by dead white men) are ever recorded. But, arguably, all the Riverside Editions of Chaucer's Collected Works should join Koestler's bust in the cupboard of academic shame.

In May 1380, the author of *The Canterbury Tales* was accused of the 'rape' of Cecilia Champaigne – and released after a payment to the lady of ten pounds (a goodly sum in the fourteenth century). Scholars debate whether the Law Latin term (Cecilia's complaint is of *'de raptu meo'*) indicates not actual rape, but abduction, or kidnap – as in the 'Rape of the Sabines'. But in support of the commoner meaning of the word, the epithet 'Chaucerian' has always carried with it, as part of its celebration of the 'bawdy', the suggestion that casual rape might be one of the inalienable rights of man – or, at least, young men, like the lusty Cantabridgian heroes of 'The Reeve's Tale', who merrily plough their way through the unconsenting womenfolk of the Miller who has given them accommodation (they *really enjoy it*, the tale implies; the victims, that is); or the knight, at the opening of 'The Wife of Bath's Tale', who violates a young maiden he encounters, as unconcernedly as a rambler might pluck a berry from the hedge.

Mention of knights recalls another violator who has a curricular presence in Edinburgh's English courses, and those of other top universities. Sir Thomas Malory wrote the hugely influential saga *Le Morte d'Arthur* while serving a long prison sentence for, among other offences, gang rape. Hardly Camelot.

These are ancient and much chewed-over matters. But in advanced academic circles there is lively debate on what is called the 'ethical classroom'. Should authors like the wife-beater Robert Lowell, the alcoholic William Faulkner, or (alleged) closet racists like Kingsley Amis and Philip Larkin, be exiled from the curriculum? Or is this the censorship of pseudo-enlightenment

– no different from the kind of bone-headed prejudice that bans *Huckleberry Finn* and *Slaughterhouse-Five* from small-town local libraries in rural America? Or the Yesodey Hatorah senior girls' school in Hackney, London, whose pupils voted in March 2008 to boycott Shakespeare entirely, on the grounds of the dramatist's perceived anti-Semitism.

It's a vexed issue. 'If only,' Mrs Humphry Ward (that most morally upright novelist) pondered, 'we had more *respectable* geniuses.' If only.

In the Dock: Ma Hump

'Ah, but what *is* respectability, Mrs Ward?' a modern Pontius Pilate might ask. The definitions change as capriciously, it would seem, as skirt length (not hers, one hastens to say).

In witness of which, the leading candidate for the least-likely-literary-junkie award (set up in memory of Bill Burroughs) is none other than Mrs Humphry Ward herself, pious author of the most successful novel of faith and doubt in the doubt-ridden nineteenth century, *Robert Elsmere*, and, as a public figure, the very epitome of all that was most respectable in Victorian England.

Afflicted with an array of neuralgic, rheumatic, dermatological, and nervous pains during her long writing career Mrs Ward ('Ma Hump', as disrespectful younger writers called the good lady) became an expert amateur apothecary and travelled everywhere with a portable medicine cabinet full of pills ('tabloids', as they were called), lotions and a 'thousand and one little drugs'. She was always keen to push her wares on to others who might be in need.

Great Writers' Little Helpers

Samuel Taylor Coleridge: opium (viz: preface to 'Kubla Khan').

Jack Kerouac: Benzedrine Nasal Inhalers (like another famous American, Jack didn't actually inhale but swallowed the active ingredients).

Honoré de Balzac: caffeine – up to forty cups of super-strength a day. When that didn't work, he would eat coffee grounds raw, Benzedrine being not yet invented, nor double-strength espresso.

Robert Southey: nitrous oxide, 'laughing gas' – 'I am sure the air in heaven must be this wonder working gas of delight', he wrote, in a transport of delight: or a trip, as it would later be called.

Aldous Huxley: mescaline – the cactoid that opened his doors of perception, confirming to him that the benignly narcotic drug 'Soma' he had imagined in *Brave New World* did actually exist.

Half-Good Samaritan, half-Dr Feelgood. 'Ma Junk', one might say.

Prominent among the author's little helpers were two Class A substances: morphia and cocaine, for the ups and downs of the writing life. Cocaine was first extracted as a chemical from the coca leaf in the 1850s. But until 1883 – when it became fashionable overnight among smart young men in Europe – cocaine was not widely available. Even medical people, such

William S. Burroughs: as his comments in the film, *Drugstore Cowboy*, imply, Dilaudid was his drug of choice. The rectal suppository was a favoured means of ingestion: 'the needle is not important'.

Jacqueline Susann: the anti-depressant Elavil was the favourite 'doll' in Jackie's valley.

Wilkie Collins: laudanum. Collins claimed to have written a sizeable section of *The Moonstone* under its powerful influence. His eyes looked like 'bags of blood', one secretary reported.

Barbara Cartland: royal jelly (the explanation for her remarkably preserved beauty in later life, she liked to explain).

Alcoholics are too numerous to mention. Numerous, too, are lovers of the illicit weed. The 'veryimportanthopheads' website lists scarcely fewer distinguished authors than *The Oxford Companion to Literature*.

as Mr Holmes in Baker Street with his 'seven per cent solution' (injected) and young Dr Freud in Vienna misconceived it as an unusual but useful, and relatively harmless, tonic (in Freud's case, the misconception had tragic results for his patients).

Mrs Ward is first found mentioning cocaine in correspondence with her mother in October 1887. It 'works like magic', she reported. Ten years later, as she tore through the bestseller lists, she was still enthusing over its 'wonderful effect'.

The First Spliff

In July 2007, the *Daily Mail* terrified parents (but probably not their delinquent offspring) with a splash front-page headline: 'Just One Joint Can Give You Schizophrenia'.

'Reefer madness' was first depicted in literature in 'The Hashish Man', one of Lord Dunsany's suggestive 'Gothic Tales'. At a London dinner party, a guest confesses his habit – and the exotic visions of the Orient which hashish brings:

> I work in an insurance office all day, and I hope you won't forget me if ever you want to insure – life, fire, or motor – but that's no part of my story. I was desperately anxious to get back to my flat, though it is not good to take hashish two days running ... When at last I got away I had a letter to write; then I rang for my servant, and told him that I must not be disturbed, though I left my door unlocked in case of accidents. After that I made up a good fire, and sat down and partook of the pot of dreams. I was going to the palace of Thuba Mleen.

One would like to think that Dunsany's 'pot of dreams' is the origin of marijuana's street name. But the dictionaries, dull dogs as ever, inform us that 'pot' more probably derives from the Mexican *potiguaya*: dried hemp leaves.

Oddly, the first wholly unexcited depiction of what one might call the social use of the drug – sharing a joint communally – is found in H. Rider Haggard's African adventure story, *King Solomon's Mines* (1885).

The Great Hunter, Quatermain, and his companions are making their arduous way to the fabulous diamond mines at the end of King Solomon's Road, feasting by night on big game. It is a relaxing time, a period for digestion, conversation, and mild pick-me-ups:

> By the time the 'scherm' was finished the moon peeped up, and our dinners of giraffe steaks and roasted marrow-bones were ready. How we enjoyed those marrow-bones, though it was rather a job to crack them! I know of no greater luxury than giraffe marrow, unless it is elephant's heart, and we had that on the morrow. We ate our simple meal by the light of the moon ... Well, there we three sat yarning away in the beautiful moonlight, and watching the Kafirs a few yards off sucking their intoxicating 'daccha' from a pipe of which the mouthpiece was made of the horn of an eland, till one by one they rolled themselves up in their blankets and went to sleep by the fire.

'Crashing', as later generations would say.

The hottentot term 'daccha' or 'dagga' is (they tell me) one of the other street names for Indian hemp. A jungle name as well, apparently. It can, one may note, also refer to the alternative narcotic, *Leonotis leonurus*. But marijuana is what it is conventionally taken to mean here.

Ironically, 'bush meat' is regarded as contraband even more culpable than C-category marijuana nowadays by HM Customs Inspectors. You have a better chance getting off with a warning, smuggling in a modest amount of 'green gold' (as, one gathers, dagga is called in South Africa) than with an elephant heart or giraffe steak secreted in your carry-on bag.

The incidence of schizophrenia among the Great Hunter's 'Kafirs' is not recorded.

LITERARY ASSAULT
AND BATTERY

The first writer to use fiction for revenge on a loathed former loved one was Lady Caroline Lamb. Caroline had the misfortune to fall in love with Lord Byron. He was, she memorably said, 'mad, bad, and dangerous to know'. Particularly dangerous for her, as it transpired.

A married woman and mother, at twenty-seven years of age, Lamb embarked on a wild, adulterous and scandalously indiscreet affair with the young poet on the eve of his 'waking famous', with the publication of his long poem *Childe Harold* in 1812. The affair lasted four months: she thereafter spent the next four years stalking, blackguarding and harassing him. Generally, as it was thought in her circle (and his), making a complete fool of herself.

Her bitterness distilled into the 'Hell hath no fury' novel, *Glenarvon* (1816), and its callously Byronic hero (Lord Glenarvon, that is). The world devoured the novel and the same world despised the luckless author for writing it. Lamb died, mentally broken down, in her early forties. Byron, whose withers were entirely unwrung by this or any other scandal in his life, termed her novel a 'fuck and publish' venture.

Byron's term was, unsurprisingly, not picked up by the Regency booktrade; although something like it emerged in the late twentieth-century with the 'Fucking and Shopping' school of fiction, pioneered by Jacqueline Susann and perfected (profitably) by Judith Krantz and Danielle Steel.

F&P novels sprout up sporadically during the nineteenth

century and comprise a small, but poisonously simmering, genre. The leading practitioner was Rosina Bulwer, whose husband had her incarcerated in a lunatic asylum for her depictions of him in ad hominem novels such as *Cheveley* (1839). Bulwer, it should be said, had hardly started the marriage off on the right foot by bringing his current mistress along on the honeymoon.

Full blooded F&P, no-holds-barred, War-of-the-Roses stuff, came into its own with the rise of the American Jewish Novelists, who took over from the Southern Novelists in the 1960s as leaders in the never-ending hunt for the fabled Great American Novel – a beast as elusive as Ahab's Great White Whale.

After his failed attempt to stab his second wife (of six), Adele, to death at a party in 1960, 'with a dirty three-inch penknife', Norman Mailer went through with the crime, in his next novel, *An American Dream*. The narrative opens with the hero, Rojack, strangling his wife before proceeding to anally rape her German maid. All in the Mailerian day, one apprehends.

The former Mrs Mailer, once recovered, declined to press charges (had she done so, the novelist would certainly have served hard time) and went on to pursue a successful career as an alternative healer. She wrote a late-life memoir, in which she recalled her version of the stabbing episode; rather more amiably than had Norman – but not without a certain spite (he had gone down tearfully on his knees, she recalled, begging her not to prosecute; so much for Mr Macho and his three inches).

Towards the end of his long career Saul Bellow wrote what many saw as a settling-of-accounts novel, *Ravelstein* (2000). A *roman-à-clef*, it jangled with so many keys (for those who knew anything whatever about the novelist's life) that one wag jested the title page should carry the statement 'any resemblance to living persons is coincidental my arse'. *Ravelstein* contains, among its gallery of easily identifiable characters from the author's past, savage depictions of former spouses. Or so it was everywhere presumed.

Claire Bloom, Philip Roth's second wife, got her post-divorce retaliation in early with the memoir *Leaving a Doll's House* – a book which was pointedly unflattering to her ex. Roth hit back with the depiction of Bloom (as it was everywhere assumed) as 'Eve Frame' in *I Married a Communist* (1998). The novel, as one reviewer put it, 'plays a chillingly mean game of "So There Claire"'. Never, as Mark Twain warned, pick a fight with a man carrying a barrel of ink. Particularly one who can spray ink as skilfully as Philip Roth.

Obviously being a member of the ex-wives' club, if your husband was an American Jewish Novelist, was dangerous. And not just for the WAJNs. Peter Carey, the distinguished Australian novelist and two-time Booker winner, broke up with his second wife, the theatre director Alison Summers who, after a twenty-year-long relationship culminating in a messy divorce, found herself at risk of being removed from the dedication pages of his novels. More hurtfully, as Summers complained, she found herself depicted, as she claimed, in *Theft: A Love Story* (2006) as an 'alimony whore'. It was, she told the *Guardian* 'a kind of intimidation. It's emotional terrorism.'

Join the club.

GUNPLAY

I teach part of the year at the California Institute of Technology: a science school. So much so, as they joke, the taps are marked not hot and cold, but acid and alkali. Although very smart in their specialist subjects, many Caltech students have little prior acquaintance with literary texts or how to criticise them. The ropes are very strange to them. They have the engaging habit of treating works of literature as if the things were lab rats.

The consequences are often oddly enlightening. On a course devoted to popular fiction of the 1970s (one can do that kind of thing in American universities) one 'Techer', on my asking him his considered verdict on Frederick Forsyth's *The Day of the Jackal* responded, bluntly, 'It doesn't work.'

On being asked why it didn't work, he pointed to chapter 14, where the Jackal secretes the custom-made gun (which can double as a walking frame) with which he will assassinate De Gaulle, by 'spot welding' the parts with a 'soldering iron' to the underside of his Aston Martin:

> For two hours he carefully welded the thin steel tubes that contained the rifle parts into the inner flange of the Aston's chassis.

There is here, my metallurgic student informed me, a process error. 'The solder wouldn't hold; welding, like brazing, is something else', the student went on to explain, with a welter of detail. The gun would simply drop off en route, even if it ever stuck. Hence, for that scientific literalist, nothing worked in the novel. It was not fiction, but busted fiction. De Gaulle would live, the lab rat (or novel) one's not so sure about.

GUNPLAY (II):
ARMS AND THE WOMAN

Which crimebuster, currently riding high in the bestseller lists, packs the most heat? The answer would have to be Patricia Cornwell's 'body farm' expert, Kay Scarpetta.

In the early novels, the feisty Chief Medical Examiner favours a Ruger .38 'loaded with Silvertips, one of the most destructive cartridges money could buy'. In later novels she has switched to a Browning 9mm with a customised Birdsong finish.

In *From Potter's Field*, Scarpetta stashes two Remington shotguns in her garage (a Marine Magnum and an .870 Express Security), along with a Glock 9mm, a Smith & Wesson, and a Colt. 'I could not deny', the lady admits, 'that by normal standards I owned too many guns.'

GUNPLAY (III):
ARMS AND THE MEN

The most flamboyantly gun-packing male hero of current popular fiction is Jack Reacher, the creation of Lee Child – 'the best thriller writer of the moment', as the *New York Times*'s Janet Maslin unreservedly calls him (alas, for thriller writers, such moments rarely last).

Reacher is ex-military, and expert in the use of lethal weapons. He was a major in the 110th special unit of the American military police. A *corps d'élite* – and ultra hard (Reacher regards the

SAS as so many Limey softies). As we first encounter him, in *Killing Floor* (1997), he's in his mid-thirties and the lonest of rangers.

Reacher has neither possessions nor family, never stays in the same town more than a few days, always travels by Greyhound bus under constantly changing assumed names. He's 6ft 5 in, 230 lbs of vagrant vigilante.

Trouble is his business. Reacher clears it up with a ruthlessness which he describes in technical detail. While gouging out a bad guy's eyeballs, the more conveniently to slit his throat, he explains: 'You don't do it with one elegant swipe. Not like in the movies. No knife is sharp enough for that. There's all sorts of tough gristle in the human throat. You have to saw it back and forth with a lot of strength. Takes a while.' Thanks for the tip, Jack.

Reacher is utterly conscienceless. Having bust one opponent's larynx (fatally) and blinded his sidekick (those thumbs again) he records feeling: 'No guilt, no remorse. I felt like I'd chased two roaches round the room and stomped on them.'

The bad guys in Reacher's universe are badder even than he is. They enjoy, for example, castrating their victims and forcing wives to eat their husbands' testicles before the sadistically delayed *coup de grâce*. Stomping is too good for the likes of them. The roach is a monarch of the glen by comparison.

Versatile as Reacher's weaponry is – thumbs, knives, boots – firearms are his specialty. One of the novels, *The Persuader*, is actually named after a shotgun whose blast is guaranteed to turn human tissue into ketchup.

As his publicists proclaim, Reacher is 'a new *American* hero'. Just like Guantanamo is a new kind of American correctional facility. No more Mr Nice Guy. Less publicised is the fact that Reacher is the creation of an English author. Child was born in Coventry in 1954, and had a worthy career in British television, before taking to fiction. After a corporate shake-up he was 'fired', aged forty, and took profitably to writing thrillers.

Child's background, ruthless and triggerhappy (in its way) as the world of British TV may be, is not one where actual gunplay is routine. He is not ex-SAS and, presumably, his weaponry expertise is, as they say in the media, 'researched', not first hand. That expertise has been questioned by the leading gun-nut website (thehighroad.org) which designated David Morrell (creator of Rambo) the 'best gun author', followed by Robert B. Parker (creator of the Private Eye, Spenser). 'Worst Gun Author', by general agreement, was Robert Ludlum. As one critic said:

> he puts safetys [sic] on revolvers, silencers on revolvers, clips on UZIs, cordite is the only propellant he has ever heard of, and when the hero picks up a revolver from a bad guy he takes his extra clips with him!! He sucks.

Child comes out with a creditable C+ for his ballistic research, although doubtless he would have the eyeballs of any gun enthusiast who gave him less than an A. But as the website records:

> The treatment Child's gunnery ranges from the impossible (Reacher cocks guns with no external hammer) to the improbable (discovers a .50 Desert Eagle that a small town Georgia detective kept as a service weapon), but the stories are great. And sometimes he even gets it right.

Forsyth, it's interesting to note, gets it wrong very rarely (let's award him B+). The only error the gun-nuts can come up with in his gunnery is a 'PPK firing 9mm parabellum in *The Odessa File*'.

Gunplay (iv):
The Hemingway Solution

The above term has become ironic shorthand for suicide by shotgun to the head, the blast directed beneath the chin, or inside the mouth. If the barrel is long, or the suicide victim's arm-reach is short, the trigger(s) can be activated by the toe. This requires taking off the shoe, of course, which militates against hasty, or impulsive, action. Anyone who employs the Hemingway Solution probably does so with considerable forethought.

The phrase has become proverbial enough in the US not to require glossing. Thus a character in Stephen King's novel *Dreamcatcher* says:

> 'Damn it, why did he have to go and use the Hemingway Solution in my room? Now there's brain matter all over my ceiling.'

This splatter for others to clear up is a main reason that Derek Humphry, the guru of 'assisted death' (i.e. suicide), urges against this particular 'solution'. If it is employed in a hotel, he suggests, leave a generous tip for room service. Thoughtful members of Hemingway's profession also give the question of mess particular thought. In *Samuel Beckett: A Personal Memoir* (2006) John Calder, Beckett's English publisher, recalls:

> One evening in 1961 when we met, the newspapers were full of Hemingway's suicide and we never got off the topic. We agreed that suicide was the best way to die, but Sam's problem was how not to leave a mess for others to clean up, while mine was how to do it quickly and painlessly.

But did Hemingway himself, in fact, employ the Hemingway solution? If one turns to wikipedia.org, one finds the following:

> Hemingway is believed to have purchased the weapon he used to commit suicide at Abercrombie & Fitch, which was then a firearm supplier. In a particularly gruesome suicide, he rested the gun butt of the double-barrelled shotgun on the floor of a hallway in his home, leaned over it to put the twin muzzles to his forehead just above the eyes, and pulled both triggers.

Time magazine (6 July 1999) offered an equally detailed, but materially different narrative:

> Next morning, shortly after 7 a.m., a pajama-clad Hemingway went downstairs and from the gun rack took his favorite gun, which, like almost everything he owned, was not merely a thing but a ceremonial object. A twelve-gauge, double-barrelled shotgun inlaid with silver, it had been specially made for Hemingway. He put the gun barrel in his mouth and pulled both triggers. The blast blew his whole head away except for his mouth, his chin, and part of his cheeks.

If it's in *Time* it *must* be true. Or so the media folklore goes.

The biographies do not entirely clear up the issue. Nor did the family. For some time after the tragedy Hemingway's widow, Mary, as keeper of the flame, insisted that her husband's death was an accident incurred while cleaning the shotgun. This cover story (which, as Mrs Hemingway later confessed, not even she believed) was given out to the press.

The fact is that so destructive, at point blank range, is the blast of the hugely powerful weapon Hemingway chose that any reconstruction of the fine detail of how he did it must be speculative. It does to the head what ketchup does to tomatoes. Mary

The First Detectives in Fiction.

Ingenuity can trace detective work back to Oedipus Rex and King Solomon's nifty forensic work in the Bible. But the first professional detective in fiction is usually taken to be the ingenious C. Auguste Dupin, in Edgar Allan Poe's 'Murders in the Rue Morgue' (1843). Dickens introduced the Scotland Yard detective, in the person of the equally ingenious Inspector Bucket, in *Bleak House* (1853, based on the real-life 'thief-taker', Inspector Field). Wilkie Collins developed the type in Sergeant Cuff, in *The Moonstone* (1868), a work which is conventionally regarded as the primal British 'detective novel'. Collins introduced the first canine detective in his late, and wholly unregarded work, *My Lady's Money* (1877). Fyodor Dostoievsky, an admirer of Dickens, pitched in with Porfiry Petrovich, in *Crime and Punishment* (1866 – it could as well be called 'Crime and Detection'). The first, and most famous, amateur detective is the immortal (literally – he proved wholly unkillable, his vexed author found) Sherlock Holmes, introduced by Arthur Conan Doyle with *A Study in Scarlet* (1888). The first Private Eye is Bozzle, in Trollope's *He Knew He Was Right* (1869). The first woman detective is usually taken to be Anna Katharine Green's doughty New Yorker, Amelia Butterworth, introduced in *That Affair Next Door* (1897).

Hemingway, who was the first to see the body at shortly after six on the morning of 2 July 1961, describes 'the shotgun lying in the disintegrated flesh'. As the biographer, Kenneth S. Lynn notes:

> The explosion blew away his entire cranial vault. Whether he had placed the gun barrels in his mouth or pressed them to his forehead is impossible to say.

There is a curious postscript to this grisly business. As Neil A. Grauer records, on his 'cigar aficionado' litblog, after the estate was cleared up, and the inheritance sorted out:

> Hemingway's sons, John, Patrick and Gregory, formed Hemingway Ltd. in 1992 to license the use of his name, image and signature. (Each son has long earned up to $100,000 a year in Hemingway-related royalties.) They came in for some heated criticism when one of the first items they authorised was a Hemingway shotgun. They protested that their father really had loved such a gun.

It is not recorded whether the Hemingway shotgun has become a Hemingway Solution weapon of choice.

8

Who? Who? Who?

'Which of you has done this?'
          Macbeth, in madness.

Who 'Wrote' *Paradise Lost?*

Putting aside *Beowulf* (essentially a German poem), the first great epic in English is *Paradise Lost.* It was a poem intended, as the poet said, to 'Justify the Ways of God to Man'. And it was, legend has it, *written* (if not actually composed) by a woman. Or, more precisely, women. Namely the blind poet's three daughters: Deborah, Anne, and Mary.

Posterity (at least its male segment) has always relished the image of the Misses Milton serving the role of dutiful pen-pushers to blind (male) genius. As the authors Sandra Gilbert and Susan Gubar put it in their polemic, *The Madwoman in the Attic*:

> Paintings of Milton dictating to his daughters were quite popular at the end of the eighteenth century and throughout the nineteenth. One of Keats's first acts on moving into new lodgings, for instance, was to unpack his books and pin up 'Haydon – Mary Queen of Scots, and Milton with his daughters in a row'. Representing virtuous young ladies angelically ministering to their powerful father, the picture would seem to hold a mirror up to the nature of one of Western-culture's fondest fantasies.

'Milton's Daughters', along with the (apocryphally) burned bras in Atlantic City in 1968 (they were actually thrown in trash cans after that year's Miss America competition) became an icon of post-1960s feminism. They symbolised the 'fond fantasy' of female subservience to male genius. As late as December 2000 Susan Sontag (herself, now, an icon) mused in the *New York Times*:

Don't we imagine that Milton's daughters, at the end of each day of the dictation of *Paradise Lost*, read it all back to their father aloud and then took down his corrections?

We, and Sontag (who seemed not to have looked into the matter), indeed have to 'imagine' it – because, in point of fact, it never happened.

As the biographers of Milton incontrovertibly inform us, Milton's daughters were probably incapable of taking down so much as a laundry list. As was common among middle-class daughters of households at the period, they could just about read. Edward Phillips (from whose account most of our knowledge of the domestic life of Milton is drawn) describes the author of *Paradise Lost* making his daughters read aloud to him Latin and Hebrew source material, of which tongues they understood not a word. The 'irksomeness' of the task, according to Phillips, led to rebellion. And worse. They stole money from their blind father and even descended to 'the despicable act of stealing his books'. Totally estranged from them at the end of his life, the father left the three women nothing in his will.

As for 'writing' one of the daughters, Anne, was so illiterate that she could not even sign her name, but had to leave her 'mark' on any document where her signature was required. Milton's motives for not educating his daughters so that they *could* have been what posterity loves to 'imagine' them as being, conduits of paternal genius, has never been explained.

Stick that on your wall, John Keats. The honour of the sex, as copyist to genius, is somewhat redeemed by Tolstoy's wife Sophie, who, reputedly, copied out the text of *War and Peace* some seven times from beginning to end. Greater love hath no spouse.

WHO 'WROTE'
THE TRAGIC MUSE?

A catch question, along the lines of the above about the Misses Milton. Henry James, of course, composed *The Tragic Muse*. But the text (or, at least, the preface) was the first thing dictated to, transcribed and typed up by James's amanuensis (or 'typewriter', as they were confusingly called), the magnificently named Theodora Bosanquet (1880–1961).

A graduate of University College London, and a self-taught agency typist, Miss Bosanquet served James from 1907 until his death in 1916, at a payment of twenty-five shillings a fifteen-hour week (just about what Anthony Trollope received, as a starting clerk in the Post Office, seventy years earlier). James approved her work, and her appearance ('boyish').

Bosanquet wrote a reminiscence of her years with the 'Master', *Henry James at Work* (1924). A pioneer feminist, she went on to serve her country as a civil servant in World War I and, thereafter, pursued a career as successful writer and editor in the London higher journalism world. A world where a woman had to be at least twice as good as a man to compete on equal terms.

An enthusiast for higher education for women, Bosanquet is commemorated by a number of bursaries and fellowships. It has been suggested that Bosanquet, a latter day 'Milton's Daughter', should get credit in the bio-bibliographical information (conventionally on the reverse side of the title page) along with the legally required information as to who printed the work.

Invisibility may be hard to counteract. Astonishingly, Bosanquet,

James's co-worker, has no entry in the revised *Oxford Dictionary of National Biography* (2004).

WHO WROTE *THE ODYSSEY*?

There is a contrarian view, originating with Samuel Butler (that most anti-Victorian Victorian), that the author of *The Odyssey* was actually an 'authoress'. The blind bard may have sung it: but a female hand first wrote it. The idea was taken up by Robert Graves (another career contrarian) in his 1955 novel, *Homer's Daughter*.

According to the Graves version, the 'writer' of the Western world's first epic was Nausicaa, 'a high-spirited and religious-minded Sicilian girl who saves her father's throne from usurpation, herself from a distasteful marriage, and her two younger brothers from butchery by boldly making things happen, instead of sitting still and hoping for the best.'

At a time when beautiful women might start wars but not write about them, the fifteen-year-old Nausicaa, as Graves conjectures, resolved to 'secure myself a posthumous life under the mantle of Homer'. She recycles the great oral work, inscribing her own, female rebalancings and inserting herself into the narrative. Unsurprisingly, she perpetrates some tell-tale gender errors (actually to be found in the surviving Homeric text). 'I put a rudder at the *prow* of Odysseus's ship', Nausicaa later discovers. What would *she*, a mere woman, know about marine engineering?

Received critical opinion is that women and epic are chalk and cheese. A much referred to college textbook, *Literature and Gender* (1996), is peremptory on the subject:

Though scholars have seriously suggested that Homer was a woman, no famous Western epic is normally attributed to female authorship.

As street criticism might say, 'it's a guy thing'.

The other error that Graves's Nausicaa confesses to having made in her authorship is that 'it takes more than two or three men to hang a dozen women simultaneously from the same rope'. This refers to that distasteful episode, at the conclusion of Homer/Nausicaa's narrative when Odysseus and Telemachus, having bloodily disposed of Penelope's suitors hang the dozen household maids who have been forced to serve the unwanted guests in Odysseus' homestead.

Before execution, using one of the ship hawsers, the two restored rulers of Ithaca, make the maids clean up the gore and guts. They are, after all, maids – even if they have lost their maid-enheads. A cleansing bow, sword and rope are quite in order for a man. A mop never.

Margaret Atwood, in *The Penelopiad* (2005) rewrites this episode from the woman's (unepical) point of view. 'The story as told in the *Odyssey*,' she claims, 'doesn't hold water: there are too many inconsistencies. I've always been haunted by the twelve maids.' These victims go on to haunt Atwood's story, and its male heroes, as an angry chorus chanting, ensemble, such taunts as:

> You roped us in, you strung us up, you left us dangling like clothes on a line. What hijinks! What kicks! How virtuous you felt, how righteous, how purified, now that you'd got rid of the plump young dirty dirt-girls inside your head!

For Atwood, the *Odyssey* could never have been written by a woman. It's a male-chauvinist-guy thing.

Who Wrote What?

In November 2007, the Oxford University Press included *Macbeth* and *Measure for Measure* in their complete edition of the plays of Thomas Middleton (the 'true' author).

In late life the illustrator George Cruikshank claimed to be the authentic author of *Oliver Twist*. Dickens was not alive to explode with contradiction.

Nancy Milford, in her biography of Zelda Fitzgerald (1970), claimed that his wife inspired a large proportion of what has been canonised under the name of her husband, Scott.

Thomas Hardy dictated his 'biography' to his second wife, Florence. It came out under her name.

Norman Fruman, in his study of Coleridge, *Damaged Archangel* (1971), observes, cattily, that the author of 'The Ancient Mariner' is the only major author whose collected works shrink every year, as scholars discover ever more material which properly belongs to other hands than Coleridge's.

WHO WROTE
THE FIRST WESTERN?

The 'guy thing' argument is inherently flawed. Critical prejudice, for example, would automatically make the same assumption about Westerns and women. Six-guns and leather chaps are things for gun-toting chaps. But *Malaeska, the Indian Wife of the White Hunter* (1860), the first 'Dime Novel' – procreator of the Western genre – was written by a woman, Ann S. Stephens.

Stephens's novel has the distinction of being 'No. 1' in Beadle's 'Dime Novel' series. The ten cent library, which would run for fifty years and, eventually, over three hundred titles, enjoyed a huge success on its launch among soldiers in the American Civil War. Dime novels would be the nursery for popular crime stories, sf and – above all – 'Westerns' in the twentieth century.

Malaeska may not have been everything its male purchasers expected. For their dime, they got a drama of racial miscegenation, which had first been published, twenty years earlier, in the *Ladies' Companion* magazine.

The novel climaxes on a note of torrid melodrama when the young hero, William Danforth, discovers that his mother is not, as he has always been led to believe, 'white', but the Indian princess Malaeska. That she is of *royal* Indian blood is no consolation. 'Great God!' he shrieks:

Dashing his hand against his forehead. 'No, no! it cannot be – I an Indian? A half-blood?'

In an excess of racial shame, he throws himself into the rushing torrent of the mighty Hudson River. Malaeska expires on his grave, 'the heart-broken victim of an unnatural marriage'.

Worth ten cents of anyone's money. Even if it is by a woman.

WHO INVENTED THE
SUPERCOMPUTER
(IN LITERATURE)?

In 1969 Arthur C. Clarke introduced the malevolent supercomputer, HAL 9000 in *2001*. He was not the first popular novelist to do so – that gold medal should probably dangle from Len Deighton's *Billion-Dollar Brain*, three years earlier. The bestselling novel and film served to familiarise the general public with the idea that these machines could be dangerous. Not just in the wrong hands, but in any hands. Ours, theirs, or just some friendly madman like Deighton's General Midwinter.

Ira Levin (author of *Rosemary's Baby* and *The Stepford Wives*) created in 1970 a dystopian vision of the future in *This Perfect Day*, in which the world is ruled – with benign tyranny – by a vast, warehouse-sized, computer called Unicomp.

None of these writers foresaw the silicon microchip, or integrated circuit – patents for which had been entered in the late 1950s and early 1960s. The future of big computers was small. And, with the arrival of the Internet, the future was not billion dollar brains, but PCs and Apples which cost scarcely more than a used microwave oven on eBay.

One sf novelist, however, vividly foresaw the Internet (devised by the American military, as a localised defence system in the late 1960s). Algis Budrys, in *Michaelmas* (1977) gets this gold medal. The idea of the Internet/World Wide Web was later familiarised to the world wide audience by 'the matrix', in William Gibson's *Neuromancer*. Published in 1984, one could only wish that the idea had been available to Orwell, thirty-five years earlier. But novelists can only foresee so far. As usual the new technology (like Orwell's telescreen) is conceived by Budrys and Gibson as an inherent tool of tyranny. Every new invention has the smell of sulphur on it.

Fiction (even science fiction) has a poor track record in scientific prophecy. Its long suit is paranoia. In this case, the evil lurking in the machine. In a thoughtful review of *Die Hard 4* in the *Los Angeles Times* in July 2007, Kenneth Turan observed that in modern popular narrative, print, TV and celluloid, the traditionally big-brained master criminal – Professor Moriarty, Ernst Blofeld, or Dr Evil – has been replaced by the all-powerful computer.

If you canvas student scientists (as my teaching commitments allow me to do) one name comes up, time and again: Vernor Vinge (pronounced 'Vin-jay'). He's the young scientists' sf writer of choice. The caviar of the genre. He's both techno-savvy and technophobic; especially where powerful computers are concerned.

Vinge himself is not young. A retired San Diego maths professor in his sixties, he writes sf with his left hand. He achieved fame, outside the sf village, with his Hugo award-winning 1992 novel, *A Fire upon the Deep*. (If you don't know who the 'Hugo' is named after, sf is not for you.)

A Fire upon the Deep is un-summarisable. It's about intellectual machinery, or AI, gone rogue. Vinge foresees thinking technologies which are no more comprehensible to the human (or sf-writing) mind than Jehova. They move in mysterious ways.

Human consciousness, whose offspring they are, can react to them, but will never understand them any more than a Pekinese can understand quantum mechanics.

This future catastrophe (for us, not the thoughtful machines) Vinge terms the 'Singularity'. He outlined it in detail in a much-reprinted article in 1993. 'Within thirty years,' Vinge predicted, 'we will have the technological means to create superhuman intelligence. Shortly after, the human era will be ended. Is such progress avoidable? If not to be avoided, can events be guided so that we may survive? These questions are investigated.'

They are investigated in his dozen or so novels. Vinge's vision of digito-apocalypse was popularised in *The Terminator*'s 'Skynet'. What happens when machines 'wake up'? Very bad things for their inventors. And no Arnie to save us.

WHO WROTE THE KING JAMES BIBLE?

Not King James. He merely 'authorised' it. KJB is the most read work of English literature ever, over the fifteen centuries we've had such a thing as can be called English literature. It is found, for example, in the drawer alongside every hotel and motel bed in the US (Norman Mailer should be so lucky). We don't normally think of it as literature – but, of course, the Bible, in this most exalted of literary forms, is an example of the English language at the highest pitch of its eloquence, subtlety and beauty. KJB was published at exactly the same period, one may note, as Shakespeare's great tragedies were being first performed at the

Globe. A main reason we tend not to think of the King James Bible as a work of literature, is because it was team-written. It is not, like most of the literature we choose to revere, the product of an 'onlie begetter' (as Shakespeare called it) an originating genius.

KJB was first published in the seventh year of King James's reign. The New Testament was translated from the Greek. The Old Testament was translated from the Masoretic Hebrew text. The finished English text was the work of six committees, utilising the expertise of fifty scholars. None the less, 80 per cent of KJB, it is estimated, is verbally unaltered from William Tyndale's pioneering English translation, produced in the earlier reign of Henry VIII. Shakespearian scholars (who must rely on printed copies produced from dubious sources often well after the playwright's death) would probably say that our texts of his works are probably only 80 per cent authentic, at best. So who wrote KJB? William Tyndale, with a bit of help, would be the soundest answer. A good copyright lawyer, did such things exist in the sixteenth century, would have made Tyndale richer than Stephen King. As it was, King Henry VIII had him burned at the stake. The two men had a difference of theological opinion about divorce.

9

Name Games

'That which we call a rose by any other name
would smell as sweet.'

Shakespeare. 'Stinkwort'?

Why 'Brontë'?

If Dr Browne, the phrenologist who read Charlotte Brontë's head (see p. 24), *had* known the name of the impressively skulled 'gentlewoman' whom he was examining that name would have struck him, as it struck most contemporaries, as very strange. The 1848 *Kelly's London Directory*, for example (the forerunner of our telephone directories and *Yellow Pages*) has no one by the name 'Brontë' ('Eyre' it does have). The origin of this curious, and wholly synthetic, surname is to be found in the tangled genealogy of the author's family.

The names 'Prunty' or 'O'Prunty', are common to this day in County Down, Northern Ireland. Charlotte's father was born there, on St Patrick's Day in 1777, of mixed Protestant and Catholic parentage. He was piously named Patrick Prunty: a name as generic in its Hibernian locality as, say, John Sutherland is in lowland Scotland.

One of ten children of a poor farming family, Patrick showed remarkable intellectual abilities which led, in 1802, to his registering as a student at Cambridge University, with a view to ordination in the Church of England. Pruntys were not common in that exalted place; particularly those with the bog still sticking to their trotters. Patrick's was an amazing achievement – as amazing as anything his wonderfully gifted children would go on to do. And, like them, he would do it early in life.

There were, however, problems with the name 'Patrick Prunty' – a name which had the same sinister resonances with English congregations as, say, 'Gerry Adams', or 'Martin McGuinness' would have 200 years later (or, come to that, 'Prunty' – it's the name of the IRA villain in the 1995 movie starring Albert Finney,

The Run of the Country). In 1798 there had been bloody uprising in Ireland, with the aim of independence, led by the 'Society of United Irishmen', encouraged by France (currently at war with England). Ireland and the Irish were not trusted, or at all liked, by the English middle classes in 1802.

At this period Patrick, prudently (given his position in the Church of England) changed his name to Brontë. He distanced himself further from his Ulster origins with a diaeresis or umlaut – a mark associated with Germany, not Ireland, a country where umlauts are as rare as the venomous snakes which St Patrick banished from the island.

Patrick, one assumes, did not want Irish baggage impeding him in his career. It was not a disgraceful thing. The Saxe-Coburgs changed their name, during World War I, to the patriotic 'Windsor', and their royal relatives, the Battenbergs changed theirs to 'Mountbatten' ('Mountbatten cake' has never quite caught on – confectioners still use the German name; 'Windsor soup' has).

There are two suggested reasons for the Rev. Brontë's choice of what his new name, and that of his children, would forever be. The word is an anglicisation of the ancient Greek for 'thunder' which, with his newly acquired classical learning, may have tickled the young Cantab's scholarly *amour propre*. He would, he might have thought, hurl thunderbolts at his errant flock. Evangelical pulpit thumping was the flavour of the age.

The more plausibly suggested reason is patriotism – to England, that is, not Ireland. Admiral Lord Nelson had been appointed Duke of Bronte in 1799 by Ferdinand, King of the Two Sicilies and Infante of Spain, grateful for the English nautical hero's exploits against Napoleon. The title was named after the town and lands of Bronte (some 3,000 acres), in Sicily, near Mount Etna (which, fancifully, may have inspired the name). A handsome estate came with the title. Short of renaming himself 'the

Revd John Bull', Patrick could not more effectively have decontaminated himself of any disloyal Hibernian affiliation.

Emma Hamilton picked up the classical allusion in 'Bronte' and teasingly took to calling her nautical lover, Horatio, 'My Lord Thunder'. The Brontë children were also consciously, or unconsciously, influenced by their father's, and their own, name change. In their Angria/Gondal 'web of childhood' stories, concocted in the long hours at Haworth Parsonage, Nelson is a hero figure, along with Wellington, Byron and Napoleon.

The surname 'Thunder' may also have seeped, insidiously, into the novel-writing daughters' sensibilities. The critic David Lodge has noted Charlotte's ('Charlotte Thunder's') love of elemental names: Jane Eyre ('air'), Helen Burns ('fire'); St John Rivers ('water'). And Emily gave English literature 'Heathcliff'. Elementalism one might say, permeates *Jane Eyre* and *Wuthering Heights*. Theirs is a thunderous climate.

On Nelson's death the Bronte title passed to his brother William. When William died he had no surviving male heir, but in accordance with Nelson's will the dukedom passed to William's daughter Charlotte. So, odd as the name is, there *is* another Charlotte Bronte. None the less, I find no one of that surname in the 2007 BT directory. 'Eyre' is, as always, common enough.

By way of curious afterthought, I cannot help noticing that if you add the umlaut to the final 'e' of 'Eyre', as the Rev. Prunty did to his new name, you get 'Eyrë' – which, phonetically, is 'Eire', or 'Ireland'. Was this a code, deliberately inserted by Charlotte – a secret affirmation of inextinguishable Celtic loyalty? Probably not. ''Twere to consider too curiously to consider so,' as Shakespeare's less thunderous Horatio says. But, while indulging over-curious considerations, would one approach *Jane Eyre* less reverently if its author were titled 'Charley Prunty'?

Title Pages that Never Were

Heart of Darkness, by Teodor Nalecz Korzeniowski.

The Naked and the Dead, by Nachem Malech Mailer.

Middlemarch, by Mary Ann Evans, also known as 'Marian', who preferred to be known socially (if somewhat less than legally) as Mrs G.H. Lewes.

I, Claudius, by Robert von Ranke (ever cross-grained, von Ranke retained his German surname while fighting for England in World War I, but wrote his post-war work as 'Robert Graves').

Nineteen Eighty-Four, by Eric Blair (some commentators suspect Orwell thought his birth name too toff-like).

The Sorrows of Satan, by Mary Mackay (who thought her birth name too lacking in glitz and invented 'Marie Corelli'. Just as well Mr Blair didn't go for 'Erich Orwelli').

Novel on Yellow Paper, by Florence Margaret Smith (later, to the confusion of bibliographers, 'Stevie').

Tartuffe, by Jean-Baptiste Poquelin.

ADJECTIVALS

The epithets 'Brontean' and 'Thackerayan' are common in critical and general discourse. I frequently use them myself and very useful they are. But, curiously, some authors' lives, lifestyles, reputations, and literary works distil conveniently into adjectivality, and others inconveniently resist conversion. Peter Conradi, for example, gets through 500 pages of his authorised life of the novelist without once using 'Murdochian'. Having read those pages, however, one has a precise idea of what the uncouth term would mean if anyone, less stylistically scrupulous than Professor Conradi, cared to invent it.

Equally curious is the diverse baggage the authorial adjectives trail behind them. Reactions are necessarily subjective. But for me 'Brontean', like 'Byronic', carries overtones of passion, explosively suppressed. 'Thackerayan', by contrast, exudes an expansive, gently gaseous, clubman ethos, richly aromatised with Havana and Madeira.

'Chaucerian' carries with it an outhouse whiff of 'bawdy' – as does 'Joycean'. 'Dickensian' conveys joviality, and the Cheerybles' *'philosophie de Noël'*. 'Shakespearian', 'Miltonic' (why not 'Miltonian'), 'Johnsonian' (why not 'Johnsonic'?) and 'Lawrentian' bespeak moral grandeur. One bends the knee before such adjectives.

Quite different are the authorial epithets which neutrally encapsulate aspects of literary style: 'Keatsian', 'Jamesian', or 'Skeltonic'. These communicate nothing about lives or personalities – merely about the fine words the authors have left us, and the peculiar nature of that finery.

Some authors, even very great authors, are curiously adjectiveless.

Why, for example, does no one ever use the terms 'Austenian' or 'Austenic'? The pallid 'Austenish' is sometimes encountered, but is barely more usable than the horrific 'Austenesque'. The lack of a handy term for the author's essence ('It is a truth universally acknowledged', etc.) handicaps Austen scholars who are forced into the kind of awkward circumlocution which would have amused their subject mightily.

The tongue rebels against 'Bunyanian', while 'Hobbesian' trickles off it quite unobstructedly. Why should the Bedford puritan's vision of the pilgrim life be thus hobbled, linguistically, while Hobbes's 'nasty, brutish, and short' picture of the human condition has unobstructed adjectival entrance into critical discourse?

Donneian? Impossible. 'Hopkinsian'? Just bearable, but rarely encountered. 'Wordsworthian', by contrast, is threadbare with over-use, while his great contemporary, the Wizard of the North, is wholly epithetless. 'Scottian' is wholly objectionable. Like Peter Conradi, I was obliged to write a biography of Sir Walter without access to any authorial epithet. It was vexatious.

'Swiftian' yes; 'Popian' no. But why not, when 'Trollopian' is so acceptable that a journal has been so named? If 'Miltonic', why not 'Drydenic' or 'Drydenian'? Vowel-ended 'Poe', 'Marlowe' and 'Shaw' convert happily into 'Shavian', 'Marlovian' and 'Poevian', but 'Defoevian' is barbarous. 'Tennysonian' yes; 'Browningian' no. If 'Dickensian' why is his young friend Wilkie, with the assonantal name, denied 'Collinsian'? His novels are quite as distinctive as those of the great inimitable.

Among the Victorian sages, 'Ruskinian', 'Arnoldian', 'Carlylean', and 'Paterian' are common currency, but not 'Millian'. 'Millite' I fancy I've encountered occasionally – but it sounds like an extremist religious sect, such as the Muggletonians.

In the twentieth-century, the Bloomsbury authors of *Mrs*

Dalloway and *Passage to India* ('Woolfian', 'Forsterian') have their nominal epithets – but very few others of recent times. 'Waughian', 'Amisian', 'Goldingian' have never caught on. With one, spectacular, exception. If the author of *Nineteen Eighty-Four* had a pound for every time 'Orwellian' is used by politicians, journalists, critics, and the general public, his estate would be richer than Ken Follett's ('Folletian'? perhaps not).

Among the twentieth-century poets, 'Yeatsian' is common-place. But never 'Audenian'. 'Eliotic' I have occasionally seen. For some reason, one doesn't like it. It's the mocking echo 'idiotic' that smears it, perhaps. There is a PhD subject here, if any hopeful research student is reading this. A Ricksian, not a Foucauldian thesis – to use the commonly used epithets for two of the age's most influential critics.

ETIQUETTERY

One of the hardest things for an (English) English teacher to get across to American students is the intricacy of our country's class system, and the subtle authorial nomenclature that under-pins it.

Honorary titles are an awful trial. Why is 'Sir Stephen Spender' abbreviated to 'Sir Stephen' but not 'Sir Spender' while 'Lord Byron' is never 'Lord Gordon'?

Rule books can help with the aristocratic handles. For the common or garden author, it is trickier, often baffling and rife with potential solecism and, for the teacher, tedious marginal correction.

Had he stayed in his native St Louis, for example, the author of *The Waste Land* (which, one suspects, he could never have written alongside the Mississippi) would have been 'Thomas S. Eliot' not as he became (along the Thames) 'T.S. Eliot'. Eliot, in fact, is in that very select corps of writers (Chaucer, Shakespeare, Spenser, Dickens) who, like public schoolboys, are generally known by surname alone (e.g., the movie *Shakespeare in Love*).

Modern feminism has yanked women, known in their own time by marital titles, into anachronistic styles: thus it is scholarly etiquette nowadays to call Mrs Gaskell, 'Elizabeth Gaskell'. She herself would, one suspects, not be pleased: she was very loyal to her William. It was amusing to see the quandaries of journalists, reporting on the 2007 TV dramatisation of *Cranford* (should they go the whole hog, and call Miss Mattie 'Matilda'? Didn't seem right, somehow).

Wikipedia, with its full name and date first line in biographical entries, is now the students' first port of call (why bother with those mausoleum-like libraries?). It is common, in undergraduate essays in the US, to encounter such barbarous formulations as: 'David Herbert Lawrence's scandalous novel, *Lady Chatterley's Lover*', or 'Herbert George Wells's classic sf novel, *The War of the Worlds*'.

Both these novelists, as the informed English book lover instinctively knows, initialised their authorial titles as 'D.H. Lawrence' and 'H.G. Wells'. Literary etiquette requires we respect their personal convention. Writers have a variety of reasons for this kind of initialisation. George Bernard Shaw preferred to be known as 'GBS' – because, it's assumed, as an Irishman he resented the deference implied in the name of an English monarch. Good enough reason.

One can guess why writers like A.L. Kennedy (who also, bafflingly, despises full-stops) initialise their authorial titles. It's for the same reason that Marian Evans called herself 'George

Eliot' or Charlotte Brontë called herself the gender-neutral 'Currer Bell'. These authors wanted to distance themselves, and their work, from 'silly novels by lady novelists', as Eliot called them. Nominal trousers would do it.

With Lawrence and Wells initialisation has a different origin, and one that links back, yet again, to the subtle, and typically inexplicable, social charge which names carry to the English ear. Both are among the greatest authors who can legitimately claim copper-bottomed working-class origins. Lawrence's father ('dad' – not 'pater', of course) was a coal miner. Lower than low: subterranean in place of work and lower still in social status.

Wells's father was a professional cricketer turned small-town (and unsuccessful) shopkeeper. Cricket has always been the most class-ridden sport in Britain. Until the 1950s there was an annual 'players versus gentlemen' match – the implication being that the professionals were not quite gents. The first non-amateur captain of the Test side, 'Len' Hutton was appointed in 1952 (it led to long-awaited victory against the Australians). Wells's 'dad', like 'Len' was no 'gentleman'.

Both Wells and Lawrence were named, miles above their social station, 'Herbert'. Such names (along with 'Cyril' and 'Cecil') have always been heavy burdens for the working-class child – guaranteeing jeers from playground pals for whom the term 'a right Herbert' is a reflexive class insult. It carries the implication (impossible to get across to American students) of 'upper- class twit', 'Lord Snooty', and 'Hooray Henry' i.e., 'Too big for your boots'.

In child- and young manhood, Herbert Lawrence was called 'Bert'. That was fine enough for the schoolyard, but not for a publishing house like Hooray Henryish Duckworth whose Edward Garnett was the young novelist's early patron. Unlike Germany, where 'Bert Brecht' sounds pleasingly Marxist, the abbreviated name is toe-curlingly 'common'. 'Bert Lawrence' would have grated horribly on the title page of *The White Peacock* (Lawrence's first published work). 'Herbert Lawrence' offended his, incorrigibly class-loyal, ear. Hence 'D.H.'.

Similar reasoning, presumably, dictated Wells's choice. It was all very well for one of his proletarian heroes, Bert Smallways, in *The War in the Air*, to be so named: but not his creator.

The first initialised authors in English seem to have been J.S. Mill and G.H. Lewes (George Eliot's consort – how odd 'G. Eliot' would sound). Why they should be so called is curious. Why, too, 'W.B. Yeats' but not 'J. Keats'? Why 'W.H. Auden' but not 'F.L. MacNeice'? Why 'E.M. Forster', but not 'V. Woolf'? It is hopeless to try and explain the anomalies – merely to impose them as a social rule. And good literary manners.

Oddly, initialisation seems to shorten the odds dramatically among contenders for the Booker Prize. Winners include:

P.H. Newby (first)
V.S. Naipaul
J.M. Coetzee
J.G. Farrell
A.S. Byatt
D.B.C. Pierre

This is, at time of writing, some 12 per cent of the total: far higher than chance would statistically predict. Take note J.B. Barnes, M.L. Amis, and I.R. McEwan. Take heart, A.L. Kennedy.

WHAT'S IN A NAME?

Google 'Sigourney' and the first zillion hits on the screen will refer you to the film star, Sigourney Weaver. Behind the unusual name, lies a rather curious story.

Susan Alexandra Weaver was born in 1949 in New York with a canteen's worth of silver spoons stuffed in her mouth. Her father was a wealthy TV producer. The life style of the Weavers was metropolitan, Upper East Side, and WASP-privileged.

Young Susan had a narrow escape at the font: her father, Sylvester L. Weaver Jr initially intended to call his daughter 'Flavia'. He had already lumbered her male sibling with the (un)Christian name 'Trajan'. He was prevailed on to not to impose the same Latinism into the name his daughter would carry through life.

A gawky girl, and embarrassingly (to herself) lanky at close on six foot, Suzie Weaver, aged fourteen, buried herself in books. She was privately schooled and – evidently – private by nature. As she recalled for an interviewer in *Time* magazine, in 1986:

> At fourteen, Susan read *The Great Gatsby* and dubbed herself Sigourney (after the unseen aunt of Gatsby's sleek-snob lady friend Jordan Baker). 'I was so tall,' Weaver declares, 'and Susan was such a short name. To my ear Sigourney was a stage name – long and curvy, with a musical ring.' For nearly a year after this self-baptism, her parents called her simply 'S', just in case the girl changed her mind, and her name, again.

She didn't. Arguably (as with 'Judy Garland', née Frances Ethel Gumm) a star was born. Or, at least, a distant glint might be glimpsed. But if *Gatsby* had to be her source, Ms Weaver should, perhaps, have opted for 'Daisy', 'Myrtle', or 'Jordan' if she wanted something less girly. If one looks at the passage in question, in chapter 3, this is what one finds:

Jordan's party were calling impatiently to her from the porch, but she lingered for a moment to shake hands.

'I've just heard the most amazing thing,' she whispered. 'How long were we in there?'

'Why, about an hour.' 'It was – simply amazing,' she repeated abstractedly. 'But I swore I wouldn't tell it and here I am tantalising you.' She yawned gracefully in my face: 'Please come and see me ... Phone book ... Under the name of Mrs Sigourney Howard ... My aunt ...' She was hurrying off as she talked – her brown hand waved a jaunty salute as she melted into her party at the door.

This incoherent remark is the only mention of the name 'Sigourney' in the book. And, alas, it is clear that the fourteen-year-old 'S' got entirely the wrong end of the stick.

Jordan, it is clear, is here adopting the formal 'English' style of addressing her aunt by her husband's name(s). This was not just etiquette in the best circles: it was standard procedure in phone books of the 1920s. The husband paid the bills, and his was the name listed.

We never find out what Jordan's aunt's first or maiden names are: she is only identified by her two marital-chattel names: 'property of Mr Sigourney Howard'. If the impressionable Ms Weaver had been reading, say, *East Lynne* by Mrs Henry Wood (née Nelly Price) she might as reasonably have re-christened herself 'Henry Weaver' – which would not, one suspects, have gone down well with the family, or later fans. Perish the thought, bookish girl that she was, 'S' might have been reading Mrs Humphry Ward.

Nominal Curiosities

For reasons no one can fathom, Jane Austen hated the name 'Richard' (see the opening paragraph of *Northanger Abbey*) and resolutely boycotted it.

J.M. Barrie invented the name 'Wendy'. Tiny cardboard houses, hamburgers, and parents have been grateful ever since.

Evelyn Waugh's first wife was named Evelyn. This is the only occasion in literature this homonymic coincidence has happened.

Florence Nightingale was, legend has it, the first woman to be so Christian-named, her parents wishing to commemorate the fact that she was born in the Italian City. Her sister, Parthenope, was unluckier. Born in Naples, she was named after that city's patron goddess.

Dickens was an early adopter of the name Florence, for the young heroine, in *Dombey and Son* (1848). How, in light of the above, he came by the name, long before the lady with the lamp became famous, with the Crimean War in 1855 is not clear.

WHAT'S IN A NAME (II)?

Taking authorial names in vain was once a robust affair. When John Dryden penned a satire on Lord Rochester (a bad man and a good poet) the nobleman hired three thugs to beat up the poet laureate in Rose Alley, off Drury Lane. A Rose Alley Memorial Award should, surely, have gone 400 years later to Jake Arnott, whose 'truecrime' novel, *Johnny Come Home*, was published in April 2006 and, alas, pulped in August 2006. Taking a name in vain was again the issue.

Arnott had made his own name with a hugely successful series of novels, adapted for TV as *The Long Firm*. They were centred on the Soho doings of gang boss Harry Starks, a thinly disguised Ronnie Kray. Luckily for Arnott, Ronnie was no longer around to administer his favoured kind of protest to those who disrespected him or his twin brother, Reggie. Namely a bullet in the 'nut'. Or, some nifty work with a machete. A cutting review from Ronnie was something no author would forget.

In *Johnny Come Home*, set in London's tin-pan alley in the 1970s, Arnott introduced a character called 'Tony Rocco': a one-time big-band singer, now an impresario and a big-time pervert in the Harry Starks mould. Alas, out of obscurity, escorted by his learned friends in wigs, emerged the real-life Tony Rocco: former big-band singer and a figure of unimpeachable respectability.

Exit Arnott's book. Exit, also, many thousands of pounds from the coffers of Arnott's publishers, Hodder and Stoughton.

Johnny Come Home was subsequently reissued with its expensive name-change. And if Jake is prudent, he will follow hereafter the example of Arthur Hailey. The author of *Airport* was in the habit of checking his characters' names against the two million listed in the Manhattan telephone directory. It resulted in villains like the hippy terrorist in *Overload* with the surreal moniker 'Davey Birdsong'. But before the 2006 court ruling, many might have thought 'Tony Rocco' fairly surreal.

Where real names are involved, an author cannot hide behind that all-purpose shield: 'any resemblance is purely coincidental'. Nor do the courts accept ignorance as a defence. If you can be shown to have injured a real-life reputation by using their name, then you will pay. The law is right alongside the Bard – he who steals my purse, steals trash. But he who steals my good name, steals all that I have.

You're safe, of course, if your named victim has no good name to lose. When Giles Foden lampooned Idi Amin in *The Last King of Scotland*, he was quite safe – even though the exiled Amin was still alive in Saudi Arabia when the book was published. Had Foden ventured to undertake an author's tour in Uganda, when Dada was still in power, the Foden liver would probably have ended up with all the others in the Amin family fridge. There are worse things than court judgements. Ask John Dryden.

The case that blazed the trail for this kind of lawsuit in the UK was that surrounding Piers Paul Read's novel *Polonaise*, published in 1976 by Secker and Warburg. Read accidentally introduced into his story an unpleasant character called Lord Derwent. The peer of the same name was not amused. Judgement went, expensively, against novelist and publisher. The lawyers and the pulping mills had a good day.

If you take on a lord, as Dryden discovered, you're asking for trouble. But even commoners can invoke the law in protection of their good names. In his black comedy, *Porterhouse Blue* (1974), Tom Sharpe introduced a TV presenter with, what he fondly thought, was a purely fictional name. He was wrong. There was, as it happened, someone so called working in the BBC. Once more the pulping mill rolled and the ritual apologies flowed.

Arnott, Read and Sharpe all perpetrated their offences unintentionally. Writers such as Evelyn Waugh, James Joyce, and Kingsley Amis took pleasure in introducing particular enemies by name into their fiction – with deliberate malice. But they did it in nooks and corners of their novels where it would have the status of a private joke for them and their mates. Too small a bone for any lawyer to get their teeth into. Ian Fleming, on the grounds that 'I need the dullest name I can find', took 'James Bond' from the author of one of his favourite coffee table books, *Birds of the West Indies*. There was no offence taken, apparently, although Fleming did get into hot water later in the Bond saga for using real names for fictional personages.

It took a long time, centuries even, before the Great British Reading Public mastered the doublethink involved in fiction's name games. Sophisticated readers that we are, we know that David Copperfield *is* Charles Dickens and that (in his dreams) Ian Fleming *is* 007 (Sebastian Faulks I'm not sure about). But, of course, they are not. Ian Fleming's testicles were never at risk from a master criminal called Ernst Blofeld.

It gets even more teasing when it becomes treblethink. The first novelist to introduce a vignette of himself, in propria persona (although not by name), into the fabric of his novel was – rather suprisingly – Tobias Smollett in *The Expedition of Humphry Clinker*. J.G. Ballard goes a step further by calling the hero of his novel, *Crash*, 'James Ballard' and the hero of his 'David Copperfield' novel, *Empire of the Sun*, 'Jim Graham' (what does 'J.G.' stand for in the author's name – you've guessed it, 'James Graham'). Which Ballard should J.G. Ballard sue J.G Ballard for, on grounds of malicious libel? Answers please to Sue, Grabit and Run.

WHAT'S IN A NAME (III)?

Jay Gatsby, with his absurdly English name, is superficially a WASP: white, Anglo-Saxon, Protestant. His blood is blue, his breeding true. Or so he claims. The first account of his background which he supplies Nick Carraway is, as Lady Archer once said of her Gatsbyesque husband's CV, suspiciously 'creative'.

He's from the mid-West, Jay tells Nick – going on to specify 'San Francisco' which is, of course, as far west as you can go without getting very wet. He was educated at Oxford. His family, he says, all died and he came into a lot of money:

> 'After that I lived like a young rajah in all the capitals of Europe – Paris, Venice, Rome – collecting jewels, chiefly rubies, hunting big game, painting a little, things for myself only, and trying to forget something very sad that happened to me long ago.'

As Nick sardonically thinks, the Bois de Boulogne rarely teems with tiger.

Later, a more accurate CV is divulged, and very bleak it is. The Great Gatsby is, by birth:

> James Gatz of North Dakota ... His parents were shiftless and unsuccessful farm people.

What is one to make – genetically – of that Gatsby = Gatz information? From the invaluable website, www.ancestry.com, one discovers that American families with the surname 'Gatz' were indeed concentrated, as the national 1920 census records, around Minnesota and Dakota (none, however, were registered in San Francisco). The name, the same website suggests, is commonly an Americanisation of the Ukrainian and Polish 'Gac'; not WASP.

But, conceivably, it is not even pure Slavic. There is lively discussion on the web (google 'Gatz' + 'Jewish' if you're curious) as to whether the hero's birth name is a version of the Jewish 'Getz' (as in the tenor saxophone player, Stan Getz; no one, alas, ever came up with the album title 'The Great Getzby' for him).

If, as is widely hypothesised, 'Jay', a common Jewish abbreviation for 'Jacob', is Jewish, it would explain why the bootlegger Meyer Wolfshiem (based transparently on the historical gangster Arnold Rothstein) makes Gatsby his heir, enriching the young man beyond the dreams of avarice.

On the extremer fringes of blogosphere, and in some of the wilder academic conferences, it is suggested there may even be African-American blood coursing through the Gatsby veins – which seems to me a speculation too curious by far.

What's in a Title?

The title of *The Great Gatsby* encapsulates the complicated feelings we have about Jay Gatsby – driven by a pointless 'dream', enriched by bootlegging wealth but, for all that (as the narrator Nick insists), 'great'. Would the novel have achieved the status it now enjoys as the most studied work in high schools and colleges across the US, had Fitzgerald retained his original titles, 'Trimalchio in West Egg', or 'The High-Bouncing Lover', or 'Under the Red White and Blue'? Luckily his editor, Maxwell Perkins, argued him out of these 'fatal' suggestions and saved his author from inclusion in Russell Ash and Brian Lake's (delightful) anthology of titular absurdity, *Bizarre Books* (1998), along with *The Girl from the Big Horn Country* (1937) and *The Fangs of Suet Pudding* (1944).

It's a pleasant speculation whether the following works would have been as successful with the reading (and, more importantly, purchasing) public had their authors retained the original titles:

> *First Impressions*
> *Hearts Insurgent*
> *Catch 18*
> *The Last Man in Europe*
> *According to Cocker*
> *The Man of Feeling*
> *The Sisters*
> *Tote the Weary Load*

Or, as the world knows and reveres them: *Pride and Prejudice, Jude the Obscure, Catch 22, Nineteen Eighty-Four, Hard Times, Lucky Jim, The Rainbow, Gone with the Wind.*

10

Readers: Distinguished and Less Distinguished

'Some books are to be tasted, others to be swallowed,
and some few are to be chewed and digested.'

Francis Bacon

SMART WRITERS, DUMB READERS

One of the heavier crosses authors have to bear is the mass of readers unworthy of them. Sad to have to say it: but true. The 'D'Oh!' factor, is ever there.

One of Isaac D'Israeli's curiosities is entitled 'literary fiction taken as fact'. The entry begins:

> When Dante published his *Inferno*, the simplicity of the age accepted it as a true narrative of his descent into hell. When the *Utopia* of Sir Thomas More was first published, it occasioned a pleasant mistake. This political romance represents a perfect, but visionary republic, in an island supposed to have been newly discovered. It was a long while after publication that many readers were convinced that *Gulliver's Travels* were fictitious.

D'Israeli ascribes these 'blunders' to the 'simplicity of the age' in which they occurred. *Gulliver's Travels*, Gullible Times; we're more sophisticated.

None the less, it may be questioned whether our age has entirely outgrown simple-mindedness. Where science and literature meet, notably, there is still a high ignoramus quotient. Even in high places.

To his novel *Enduring Love* (1997), for example, Ian McEwan affixed a bibliography of ostensibly authentic psychological references, authenticating the mania of the stalker Jed (whose love is not the kind you want to endure). Specifically McEwan cited an article on 'de Clérambault's Syndrome', published in the *British Review of Psychiatry*, by Robert Wenn and Antonio Camia.

Not just reviewers, but qualified psychologists, took McEwan's citation at face value. In fact, the journal, the article, and the authors were as fictional as the novel's hero and heroine – or Lilliput. It created fine critical comedy. The *New York Times* reviewer loftily complained that the article indicated 'insufficient imagination' in the novel; McEwan's fiction, the paper's readers were instructed, was sadly hobbled by fact.

The gullibles were principally American. A whole batch of reviewers in eminent places – such as the *Washington Post* and the *Los Angeles Times* – when questioned by *Salon* magazine, came clean. They had been fooled by the cod article. They included, as it happened, *Salon* magazine's own reviewer, Elizabeth Judd, who had declared that stapling the stalker's fixation so precisely to an actual research paper 'saps the story of its energy'. She, alas, was the sap, as she sportingly confessed.

Being bamboozled by de Clérambault Syndrome is forgivable. More so since there was a French psychiatrist of that name, who did indeed give his name to an erotomaniac syndrome which is sometimes cited in high-profile stalking cases. It was the research paper, and the refinements of the syndrome which it elaborated (relevant to the intricate machinery of McEwan's plot) that had been fabricated.

Where the factuality/fictionality is less abstruse, the bamboozlement can be rather more shameful. Disqualifyingly so, if you set up to judge fiction in public places for the benefit of the reading public, one might think. If, that is, one did not make so many mistakes of the same kind oneself.

In 1969, George MacDonald Fraser published the first of his *Flashman* books. Inverted Victorianism was the gimmick. Instead of Thomas Hughes's Thomas Brown (that middle-class prig who, as the prelude to *Tom Brown's Schooldays* states, was principally responsible for colouring so much of the globe imperial red), Fraser told the story of the British empire through Flashman, the dandy-cad who roasts young Tom over the dormitory fire and is, to the relief of decent Rugbeians, expelled by the fearsome Dr Arnold (the most eminent of Lytton Strachey's eminent Victorians) for drunkenness and worse, hinted-at, dissipations. Fraser was intending amusing travesty. For most, but not all, readers he succeeded.

Fraser described the long-delayed acceptance, publication, and eventual runaway success of *Flashman*, and its many sequels, in an interview published in the *Daily Telegraph* (15 October 1994).

> By 1968 I was ready to call it a day but ... the novel found a home at last with Herbert Jenkins [i.e., the publisher], the manuscript looking, to quote Christopher MacLehose [i.e., the editor], as though it had been round the world twice.
>
> They published it as it stood, with (to me) bewildering results. It wasn't a bestseller in the blockbuster sense but the reviewers were enthusiastic, foreign rights (starting with Finland) were sold, and when it appeared in the US one-third of forty-odd critics accepted it as a genuine historical memoir, to the undisguised glee of the *New York Times*, which wickedly assembled their reviews. 'The most important discovery since the Boswell Papers,' is the one that haunts me still, for if I was human enough to feel my lower ribs parting under the strain, I was also appalled, sort of ... I'd never supposed that it would fool anybody. Nor did Herbert Jenkins. And fifty British critics had recognised it as a conceit.

Time magazine (5 September 1969) slightly modified the statistics, but not so as to spare American blushes:

no fewer than ten out of forty-two [American] reviewers – one of them a professor at Fairleigh Dickinson University – have been gulled into taking Flashman seriously as a real historical character.

Quis custodiet ipsos custodes? American custodians, that is.

DUMB READERS (II)

Authors sometimes try the experiment of de-naming their books. Trollope wrote a couple of volumes, anonymously. Without his name, they flopped. Doris Lessing wrote a novel in the 1980s, *The Diary of a Good Neighbour*, under the pseudonym, 'Jane Somers'. Although her reputation was sky-high at the time, it was turned down by the best publishers in London. Professional readers, manifestly, can be as dumb as anyone else. 'Too depressing' one of them informed the disgusted Lessing. Depressing indeed.

Gender-japes (so to call them) raise the stakes and make dumb readers look even dumber. In 1987, the feminist publishers, Virago, eagerly accepted a collection of stories by a young Muslim woman, Rahila Khan, entitled *Down the Road, Worlds Away*. The entire print-run (as they desperately hoped) was pulped, when the author was discovered to be not a young Muslim woman, but a middle-aged Anglican vicar based in Brighton, the Rev. Toby Forward. Of course, once that fact was known, everything fell into place. There had, every-one in the office now agreed, always been something not quite right about 'Mrs Khan'. Twenty-twenty hindsight, as the Americans say.

The most successful – and still wholly mysterious – trans-gender hoax was that perpetuated by the Victorian novelist and man of letters, William Sharp. A bearded, hearty fellow, with a background in banking and a modest reputation in manly enough novels under his own name, Sharp invented an alter ego 'Fiona Macleod' in 1894. Allegedly authentic, this entirely fictional Celtic genius seems to have taken over Sharp Edward Hyde-style. He insisted she was a real person and may even have convinced himself of the fact. He gave her a separate entry from his own in *Who's Who*, where her birthplace is given as the Hebrides, her first language Gaelic, and her recreations 'sailing, hill walks, listening'. Fiona Macleod wrote sixteen bardic novels. She could never, to the frustration of her many admirers, be lured from her secluded residence in Iona. Public appearances in Edinburgh or London would invariably be cancelled at the last minute.

The charade was sustained up to Sharp's death, in 1905. And after. Fiona Macleod's collected works were posthumously (post-William Sharp, that is) edited by their fraudulent creator's widow. Mrs Sharp was probably one of the very few in on one of the greatest literary hoaxes in history (unless, that is, the Baconians, Oxfordians or Marlovians come up with clinching evidence that Shakespeare was not Shakespeare).

Why did Sharp do it? As I say, it's mysterious. My hunch is that it was to demonstrate how sharp, indeed, he was and how dumb the Great British Public – not to mention those know-all reviewers – were. If so, William Sharp proved his point. Sharply.

PRESIDENTIAL READERS

Osama Bin Laden is not renowned as a humorist. Few mass-murderers have been. But on one of his 2004 videotapes from the North-West Frontier he got in a shrewd wisecrack against his great Satanic enemy. George Bush, he sneered, was poring over *The Pet Goat* story book while his (Osama's) people were 'ramming' the Twin Towers. Ho ho.

Perhaps in response to Osama's sneer, when the President went on his summer vacation in 2006, his office released the factoid that packed in his suitcase, as his beach book, was Albert Camus's novel *The Stranger* (also anglicised as *The Outsider*).

It seemed an odd choice of beach-book. Hard to imagine this particular president wrestling with the intricacies of being and essence while reaching for the Coppertone. But, as commentators noted, the hero-narrator in *The Stranger*, Meursault, kills (on a beach, no less) an Arab: for little other reason than he feels like it. 'Get me something about killing Muslims, godammit!' one can fantasise Mr Bush saying.

Presidential reading of fiction inevitably kindles the electorate's curiosity – offering, as it does, a furtive peek through the White House bedroom window. Theodore Roosevelt, that most can-do of presidents, was so shocked by what he read in his proof copy of Upton Sinclair's exposé of the Chicago meat-processing industry, *The Jungle* (1906), that he sent special agents to investigate whether that appetising pastrami sandwich he ate for lunch indeed contained rat and, *horribile dictu*, the odd scrap of human flesh (yes, it turned out). A clean-meat act ('Pure Food and Drug Bill') was rushed through and the President coined, in honour of Sinclair, a critical term which has been in useful circulation ever since: 'muckraker fiction'. Sometimes misunderstood in the UK, it's a term of praise. Where there's muck, there's good investigative writing.

Sinclair, a rabid socialist (something Roosevelt did not at all go along with), took a jaundiced view of this éclat. 'I aimed at the public's heart, and by accident I hit it in the stomach,' he said. A presidential stomach, as well. He wanted revolution, not better pastrami.

The novels presidents don't like, of course, are even more interesting than those they do. Roosevelt regarded Henry James as an anglicised 'poodle'. Later American presidents, of course, would have a use for the English poodle – particularly if they were Prime Ministers called Tony Blair.

Eisenhower was said to kick back, after settling the Soviet Union's hash, with the cowboy stories of Zane Grey – which seems appropriate. The old general embodied the traditional values of those riders of the purple sage.

Ike's successor, John Kennedy, famously gave Ian Fleming's career an international boost when he named James Bond as favourite reading to *Life* magazine. Kennedy was, in fact (like Roosevelt and Sinclair) what the trade calls an 'early adopter'. While still a senator, in 1957, recovering from a cold, he asked his friend, Marion Leiter, for some relaxing reading. She sent across a first novel by a new British thriller-writer everyone was talking about, *Casino Royale* (a generous woman, she also loaned her name to Fleming's unflatteringly dumb CIA operative, Felix Leiter).

Many of Fleming's bizarre wartime schemes, when he was in military intelligence in World War II, coming up with hare-brained scenarios with his AU30 unit, have an eerie similarity to the CIA's plans to kill Fidel Castro with an exploding cigar.

Bill Clinton, unsurprisingly, made known his liking for the detective stories of the African-American/Jewish crime writer Walter Mosley. In 1992, campaigning for what would be his first term, he was seen carrying a copy of *Devil in a Blue Dress* (1990). Mosley's Easy Rawlins stories (very good they are, by the way) are permeated with 1960s, 'Great Society', liberalism. Blue dresses, of course, would later prove devilish unlucky for Clinton. It was that intimate presidential DNA on Miss Lewinsky's blue dress that brought him to grief in 1999.

Unfinishables

A teletext survey, in March 2007, found the following as the top-ten novels least likely to be finished by readers embarking on the reading of them:

1. *Vernon God Little*, D.B.C. Pierre
2. *Harry Potter and the Goblet of Fire*, J.K. Rowling
3. *Ulysses*, James Joyce
4. *Captain Corelli's Mandolin*, Louis de Bernières
5. *Cloud Atlas*, David Mitchell
6. *The Satanic Verses*, Salman Rushdie
7. *The Alchemist*, Paulo Coelho
8. *War and Peace*, Leo Tolstoy
9. *The God of Small Things*, Arundhati Roy
10. *Crime and Punishment*, Fyodor Dostoievsky

All the works were concurrently cited in various 'greatest ever' and 'must read' surveys.

PRESIDENTIAL READERS (II)

In office, Ronald Reagan was very taken by the technothrillers of Tom Clancy. As that author's webography proudly recalls:

A woman in Washington, DC, read his novel *The Hunt For Red October* when it was first published by the Naval Press Institute in 1984, and loved it so much that she gave a copy to all her friends. One of those friends was President Ronald Reagan, who stepped off Marine One with the book tucked under his arm. A reporter saw the book and asked Reagan, 'What are you reading?' Reagan then held up the book so everybody could see the cover and replied, 'It's a really good yarn.' After Reagan's compliment, Tom Clancy's first novel became a best seller.

The 'yarn' which most influenced the Great Communicator, however, was of much older vintage than Clancy. Somewhere on a bookshelf in the Ronald Reagan Memorial Library, there must be a battered, much thumbed copy of Harold Bell Wright's *That Printer of Udell's*. If not, there ought to be.

Wright (1872–1944) was a Baptist minister whose first best-seller (of eighteen), was initially designed to be read aloud, Sunday by Sunday, to his Ozark congregation. 'Plain food for plain people,' Wright called his sermonical novel. Such fare was to the public taste in 1903. In the first quarter of the twentieth century, Wright's fiction outsold all others. Nowadays readers confuse him with the pioneers of manned flight, Orville and Wilbur, whose Kitty Hawk took to the skies in the same year that Harold's novel made it to the top of the newly introduced American bestseller list. 1903 was a good year for Wrights.

That plainest of presidents credited *That Printer of Udell's* as having changed his life. To a descendant of the author's, Jean Wright, who wrote to him in March 1984, he replied:

It is true that your father-in-law's book, indeed books, played a definite part in my growing-up years. When I was ten or eleven years old, I picked up Harold Bell Wright's book, *That Printer of Udell's*, which I'd seen my mother reading, and read it from cover to cover ... *That Printer of Udell's*, had an impact

> I shall always remember. After reading it and thinking about it
> for a few days, I went to my mother and told her I wanted to
> be baptised ...

Thus was the conqueror of the Evil Empire set on his path of righteousness.

Wright's narrative is a mixture of Horatio Alger's rags to riches fables, and Sheldonian, *In His Steps* pietism (see p. 98 and pp. 226–7). The hero, Dick Falkner, is orphaned early in life. His father was an alcoholic, his abused mother died wretchedly, and he now faces the world alone. He drifts into 'Boyd City', where everyone (including the church) turns him away, except for the printer, George Udell, the town 'infidel', ironically.

Falkner works hard, becomes respectable, a 'true Christian' and a tireless friend to the unemployed and vagrant classes – offering self-help, not hand-outs.

He saves young ladies (including his future wife) from sin and is a one-man social security system for Boyd City. In five short years (about the time of a presidential term, one may note) he transforms Boyd City into a place God can smile on. In the last pages of the novel, he goes into politics to do the same for America. Inspirational.

As a postscript to this riff on Reagan, one may speculate – fancifully – about what Osama Bin Laden's favourite novel might be, up there in the dank caves of Waristan. Tom Clancy returned Reagan's compliment to *The Hunt for Red October* by dedicating the follow-up Jack Ryan adventure, *Executive Orders*, to the ex-President, in 1996. The novel is remarkable in that it opens with a Washington in which the President and most of his adminis-tration have been killed by a terrorist-hijacked jumbo-jet doing a kamikaze raid on the Capitol. It's not recorded whether Osama

Bin Laden read the work. Someone in his entourage perhaps did.

PRIME-MINISTERIAL READERS

British Prime Ministers also have their interestingly favourite novels. Disraeli, of course, actually wrote his. They were, one gathers, not best liked by his mighty antagonist, Gladstone, whose favourite novel was, to judge by the 10,000-word review he gave it, *Robert Elsmere*, by Mrs Humphry Ward. Posterity, alas, has not agreed with Gladstone's literary judgement. On Ireland, the Grand Old Man was much sounder.

In the twentieth century, Macmillan's family published Thomas Hardy, but Harold Macmillan, in office, was a famed lover of Anthony Trollope – notably the 'Parliamentary Novels'. One would like to think he got some tips from Trollope's Prime Minister, Plantagenet Palliser (whose policy, as endorsed in *The Prime Minister*, can be summed up as 'the less a premier does the better for the country').

Prime Minister Stanley Baldwin was an enthusiast for the 'blood, mud, and gloom' novels of Mary Webb, and did all he could to popularise them, and her. Alas, she lives only as the novelist wittily lampooned in Stella Gibbons's *Cold Comfort Farm*. A sad immortality. John Major – like Macmillan (and perhaps inspired by 'SuperMac') – cited Trollope's *The Way We Live Now* as his favourite novel. Mrs Thatcher thought better of Jeffrey Archer the novelist than the pretender to cabinet rank. Her most famous slogan – 'The lady's not for turning' – was derived from the everywhere forgotten verse drama of

Christopher Fry, and his 1948 play *The Lady's Not for Burning*. The allusion passed most of her audience by. Nor, alas, did it raise Fry from critical oblivion.

Tony Blair, allegedly, has Scott's *Ivanhoe* in pride of place on his bookshelf. One has to believe him: he's a pretty straight kind of guy.

Gordon Brown, biographies suggest, has no time for fiction. Whether the country is better or worse for that, only history will tell. At the London Book Fair in April 2008 he indicated a certain fondness for *Catcher in the Rye,* which, one suspects, he must have read as a student at Edinburgh in the 1960s before more serious issues came to preoccupy him.

II

Mammon and the Book Trade

'Good morning to the day; and next, my gold!
Open the shrine, that I may see my saint.'

Volpone, Ben Jonson

PRODUCT PLACEMENT

'Product placement' – putting commodities into novels with a commercial motive – is a recent literary practice. It took some time for the creators and producers of fiction to realise that there was money to be had from strategic alliances with Mammon. Ian Fleming, for example, associated James Bond indelibly with the secret agent's Balkan Sobranie cigarettes, made up specially for him by Morland's in Grosvenor Street (see p. 83). But Fleming never seems to have realised Bond's trademark ciggies might be a useful source of subsidiary income.

Fleming was an innocent about 'downstream exploitation'. The Bond film franchise is not innocent. In the movie *Licence to Kill*, for example, the Lark brand of cigarette (not Balkan Sobranie) figures centrally in the plot. The then-Bond, Timothy Dalton, went on to make a commercial for the Japanese cigarette, in full 007 dinner-jacketed fig. Screw brand loyalty – they were paying big yen. Balkan Sobranie weren't offering a single dinar.

A number of companies have since led the way in placing commercial products in fiction. Most publicised is the Italian firm, Bulgari jewellery, who commissioned Fay Weldon, in 2001, to write what became *The Bulgari Connection* (in the circumstances, a wonderfully wry, Ludlumesque, title). The plot bore a close relationship to Weldon's best-known work, *The Life and Loves of a She-Devil*. Big money was paid – £18,000 in return for at least a dozen product mentions. It was clearly enough to buy one of the country's most respected writers. Weldon shrugged off all criticism. When asked how she, shortlisted for the Booker, could sell out in this way she replied that the buggers had never actually given her the prize.

At least Bulgari came through. Like Salman Rushdie, Weldon had begun working life in advertising. She didn't see it as Satan's work. The inventor of the 'go to work on an egg' slogan didn't see why she shouldn't wear Bulgari as she went to work on the typewriter. Let those fingers dazzle.

A younger and less hard-boiled market than Weldon caters for is a more attractive target for the product placers. In March 2004, The Ford Company announced that it was 'getting into Chick Lit', having recruited Carole Matthews to feature 'Britain's best-selling small car' the Ford Fiesta, in her 'fantastic new novel for young women, *The Sweetest Taboo,* when it hits bookstores next month'. Flossie the Fiesta duly starred. Whether the country's Bridget Joneses flocked to Ford showrooms is not recorded. More likely they kept their weather eye open for the hunk with the hatchback.

In America the cosmetic manufacturer, Cover Girl, took aim at the same teen market. In 2006 they commissioned Jordan Weisman and Sean Stewart, authors of the young adult novel *Cathy's Book: If Found Call (650) 266-8233* to remove all pre-existing references in their text to cosmetics, and replace them with Cover Girl's proprietary products, such as 'Lipslicks'. Weisman and Stewart's fiction is duly slicked with such references.

As reported in the *New York Times* on 12 June 2006, no fee was paid. The authors of *Cathy's Book* were not writing for hire, like Weldon. By way of a fee, Cover Girl's parent firm, Procter & Gamble, undertook to push the book on their website, www.Beinggirl.com. On the strength of this deal, the print run of the novel reportedly shot up from 30,000 to 100,000.

PRODUCT PLACEMENT (II)

Bill Fitzhugh, in an article in the *Guardian* (6 November 2000), proclaimed himself as 'the first novelist to use product placement in a work of fiction' – and, he defiantly insisted, he was proud of it:

> If, in the final accounting, I am remembered for nothing else, at least I will be remembered for being the man who ruined literature once and for all . . . The ruination of the literary form known as the novel has been laid at my feet, so bugger off.

To promote his novel *Cross Dressing* ('a satire on religion and advertising') Fitzhugh was keen to come up with a promotional gimmick that would catch the attention of the American public. As he recalls:

> An idea hit me. I had sold the book's film rights to Universal Studios. Universal (at the time) was owned by Seagrams. Two calls resulted in a deal wherein I would replace generic references to drinks with Seagrams' products.

He decanted their Scotch into the novel, Fitzhugh recalls, for publicity, not cash.

In point of fact, Fitzhugh is historically wrong. The first novelist to do product placement was Mrs Humphry Ward (dear old Ma Hump again) in 1910, in *Canadian Born* (subtitle: *Lady Merton, Colonist*). The Canadian Pacific Railway gave the English novelist a free, first-class ride, across their great country in return for a novel about an English aristocrat, who falls in love with a handsome young Canadian railway engineer en route. Mrs Ward did the CPR proud – going even further, puffing the hotels in which she, luxuriously and free-of-charge, broke her journey. The novel flopped disastrously. But she got a good holiday out of it.

Despite such straws in the wind, product placement has only very recently become a feasible literary-commercial project. The contemporary novel, it seems, is now at the same inaugural point that film was in 1982, when Steven Spielberg, as one has been told, decided to ask whether M&M (owned by Mars), or Reese's Pieces (owned by Hershey), would pay most to have their tasty product featured as the bait which lures ET out of the cupboard. Hershey won although, with its extraterrestrial name, the other manufacturer really should have done.

Spielberg, as critics note, has since gone overboard in the product placement department. In the 2002 film *Minority Report* (whose extended chase sequences transport Tom Cruise from a shopping mall to a Toyota factory to a bill-boarded freeway) it was hard for audiences to work out where the Pearl & Dean advertisements ended and Spielberg's narrative began.

The verdict is crystal clear. Readers, like movie-goers, tolerate product placement, so long as it is not obtrusive. They hate having their nose rubbed in a product. Go too far and the consumer turns.

There was, for example, resentment among the author's loyal fans at what they perceived (perhaps unfairly) as 'blatant' Mercedes Benz product placement in James Patterson's 2006 thriller *Cross*. Patterson's detective hero is described not just buying, but repeat-edly eulogising the MB R350 sedan mid-crime-busting. Bloggers reflected cynically on the novelist's automobilist enthusiasm. Was this product placement – or genuine motorist's enthusiasm? Mr Patterson has not chosen to enlighten us.

There's Life in the Old Corpse Yet

Like El Cid, as immortalised by Charlton Heston, writers some-times ride out after death, to win a literary battle or two. The website www.allbookstores.com lists some 200 authors who have 'written' posthumously.

Riding high on the list is Louis L'Amour. The author of *Hondo* (his most famous work, and John Wayne's favourite Western), Louis L'Amour's 115 titles was a solid life-time score: more so given the fact that his writing career did not start in earnest until his forties.

The writing did not stop when his life (a generous eighty-year span) ran out. An admirably methodical writer, L'Amour had apparently left several outlines and unpublished stories at the time of his death in 1988. Volumes of L'Amour Westerns were still appearing a decade and a half later to howls of rage from purist fans, who regarded these works as literary grave-robbing.

However, the outright winner in the literary El Cid stakes must be V.C. Andrews. Cleo Virginia Andrews (she later transposed her first two names) was born in 1923 in Virginia – a region she loved and where, after an unsettled life, she chose to be buried (hence the transposition of first names; she may also have died virginal – there are numerous hints in her work on the subject).

As a teenager, Virginia fell down the stairs at her school, incurring horrific spinal injury, She would be handicapped for life – needing crutches and a wheelchair in her later years. After her father died, she lived with her widowed mother, supporting the household as a commercial artist.

Allegedly Andrews destroyed her first complete manuscript, because it was too 'personal'. According to devotional websites, 'in 1972, she completed her first novel, *The Gods of the Green Mountain*, a science-fantasy story.' The work is currently available only as an e-text. In 1972 Andrews was in her fiftieth year, and by now almost wholly disabled.

But her writing hand wasn't. Between 1972 and 1979, she completed nine novels and twenty short stories, of which only one would see the light of publication: 'I Slept with My Uncle on My Wedding Night'. Or was it published? It has never been located, and is hunted by fans as the Andrews El Dorado. The third most-asked question on www.completevca.com/faq.shtml is, 'Where can I find a copy of "I Slept with My Uncle on My Wedding Night"?' Where indeed.

Incest would be a principal theme in her subsequent fiction. Or as Andrews herself quaintly put it, 'unspeakable things my mother didn't want me to write about'. Unspeakable, perhaps; but not unwritable. Or, finally, unpublishable. Andrews at last broke into print with a paperback original, *Flowers in the Attic*, published in 1979 by Pocket Books. She was fifty-six years old.

Originally entitled 'The Obsessed', the manuscript was hugely overlong, and required to be hacked into shape by the publishers. The 'uncut' version awaits publication. *Flowers in the Attic*, which attracted a measly advance of $7,500, tells the story of the four attic-incarcerated (and sexually adventurous) Dollanganger children. The novel derives, clearly enough, from *Jane Eyre* – both the Red Room (in which young Jane is incarcerated) and the madwoman in the attic hover over the narrative. Anne Frank is also there somewhere. A sad brew.

Andrews is credited with founding a distinct new line of gothic fiction: the 'children in jeopardy' genre. The term was taken over by the social service industries in the US and Britain and evolved, after a decade or two, into 'misery memoirs' (as they are known) of *The Boy Called 'It'* and *Daddy, Please Don't Hurt Me Again* kind. Harry Potter, as an abused waif in his cupboard under the stairs at Privet Drive, began his fictional life as a child in jeopardy. A Flower in the Closet.

Flowers in the Attic went on to be a bestseller: the first of a whole string of sagas revolving around clusters of (typically) children in jeopardy. V.C. Andrews had begun late as a best-selling author and finished sadly early. Seven years after *Flowers in the Attic* was published she died of cancer aged sixty-two, a year before the release of the film of her novel in which she has a non-speaking cameo; she had always longed to be an actress.

But her career did not die with her. Novels kept on pulsing out after her death under the auspices of the estate. An unceasing flow of authentic Andrews was promised – and there could never be enough of it for her fans. Allegedly Andrews had left some sixty scenarios at the time of her death. The family announced it was working 'closely with a carefully selected writer' to midwife the latent Andrews *oeuvre* into print. And they would, of course, be *her* novels – as much so as *Flowers*.

The identity of the 'carefully selected writer' was kept strenu-ously secret, so as not to contaminate the Andrews brand with another name. Many of the author's devoted readers, of course, had not apprehended she wasn't alive and writing the 'Andrews' novels which continued to pour out with only her name on the cover. By 2007, the count had reached something over seventy titles – two-thirds of which have come out under the trade-marked V.C. Andrews brand.

The ghost in the Andrews machine was, after some years, discovered to be Andrew Neiderman. His name does not appear on the copyright pages. His website www.neiderman.com makes no mention of the Andrews connection. His best-known work is the novel *The Devil's Advocate*, which was made into a popular film, starring Keanu Reeves and Al Pacino. It is about an idealistic young lawyer, who sells his soul to the devil. But no one must know.

Apparently to this day the most asked question on the Complete V.C. Andrews website is 'Where can I write to V.C. Andrews?'

'In the Attic' – a Vulgar Error

Flowers in the Attic, like the influential feminist literary-critical treatise, *The Madwoman in the Attic* (1979), by Sandra M. Gilbert and Susan Gubar draw, in their separate ways, on the supposed incarceration of Bertha Mason (the first Mrs Rochester) in the attic at Thornfield. The image has become emblematic of the historical oppression of woman. In fact, as Michael Mason points out in his 1996 edition of *Jane Eyre*: 'This is, strictly speaking, an error, since Bertha Rochester is locked up on the third storey of Thornfield Hall, and there is a "garret" or "attic" floor above.' Long live strictness.

LIES, DAMN LIES, AND BESTSELLER LISTS

There was, for students of book history, a highly informative trial in Los Angeles in the summer of 2007. On one side, the bestselling novelist, Clive Cussler. On the other side, Crusader Entertainment, a film production company owned by Philip Anschutz (recall Millennium Dome, recall John Prescott).

At issue was the film-of-the-book *Sahara*, one of Cussler's rollicking 'Dirk Pitt' series. The hope was that the movie adaptation would launch a series to rival George Lucas's Indiana Jones. Alas, no. The film bombed – despite many exciting glimpses of a semi-dressed Penelope Cruz. According to the *Los Angeles Times* the film was, two years on, still $105 million in the hole. According to the trade magazine, *Variety*, it was 'approximately $60 million'. What's $45 million between friends? Let's be approximate.

Cussler alleged that the producer ignored his authorial know-how and 'gutted' his book. Crusader blamed *Sahara*'s failure on Cussler having misrepresented to them his mass-audience appeal. 'He lied' their lead attorney, Alan Rader, bluntly alleged. Lied, that is, about his sales.

As a newspaper report put it: 'Cussler told Crusader that his Dirk Pitt novels had sold more than 100 million copies. Crusader alleged that the correct figure was 35 million, based on royalty reports and accounting figures.' What's 65 million between friends?

If, after the trial (whose outcome was inconclusive), one went to Cussler's website, sponsored by his publisher, Simon & Schuster, there was no surrender. 'Clive Cussler' we were (still) told 'is acclaimed worldwide as the Grandmaster of Adventure, a title richly deserved given that there are nearly 100 million copies of his bestselling Dirk Pitt novels in print.' Mr Rader isn't on record as acclaiming.

Sidney Sheldon died in 2007. If one goes to his publisher-sponsored website (now his cyber-tombstone) the shoutline is: 'Over 300 million books in print. The world's master storyteller.' Chew on that, Cussler.

In this muscle-flexing world Sheldon is by no means the biggest potato. In 2002, when Stephen King received a National Book Award, their official NBA press handout declared that 'more than

High and Low Earners

In November 2007, Ken Follett's forthcoming trilogy, *The Century*, was reported as having landed deals to the value of $50 million. This, to date, was the largest advance payment ever promised to a novelist.

The entire and perpetual rights of John Milton's poem, *Paradise Lost*, was purchased ('by a poor bookseller, near Aldersgate') for £10. It later yielded his widow a further £8 for the outright sale of the property.

In 1995, Jeffrey Archer signed a deal with the publisher Collins that was reported to be worth £14 million, for three novels.

The Brontë sisters' first volume of poetry sold two copies, and earned the authors less than nothing (it was vanity

300 million copies of his books are in print'. He must be worth at least a Sheldon and a half, or five Cusslers by now.

The master of horror should not rest on his laurels. John Grisham gave the commencement address at the University of Virginia, May 2007. It's a signal honour for a popular novelist to be so honoured at Jefferson's institution. But he's earned it. The college website informed us 'there are currently over 225 million John Grisham books in print worldwide'. Grisham hit the best-seller trail ten years later than King and is moving up very fast. The crown may yet pass.

published – although sales can have done little for vanity at Haworth).

Judith Krantz received a then record-breaking advance of $5 million for the primary and paperback rights to her sex-and-shopping romance, *Princess Daisy*, in 1980. It was her second novel.

Most publicised payment for the subsidiary rights to a work of fiction was the $1 million paid by Samuel Goldwyn, to Damon Runyon, for the film of *Guys and Dolls*. An image of the cheque was splashed across the opening credits of the 1955 movie.

George Eliot was promised a then record £10,000 for her historical novel, *Romola* (1863). In the event, she wrote less than contracted for, and was docked £2,000. The first true ten-thousand-pounder was Benjamin Disraeli's *Endymion* (1880).

But can either of these big hitters reach the total of the Lady in Pink, Barbara Cartland, who, we are informed (on www.condor-sj.com), 'is the most widely read author in the world with more than 500 million books in print'?

'Oh no she's not', retorts a 2007-launched website devoted to Agatha Christie (www.agathachristie.com). It's the Queen of Crime, not the Queen of Romance, who rules: 'Agatha Christie remains the most popular novelist in history', the fan-site informs us, 'with over two billion of her books sold at a conservative estimate.' Conservative?

A strong smell of fish comes off these handsomely rounded figures. The moral is, not all the fiction in fiction is contained within the covers.

WHAT WAS THE MOST POPULAR NOVEL IN THE AMERICAN CIVIL WAR?

Automatically, one hazards *Uncle Tom's Cabin* – recalling Abraham Lincoln's tribute that he wanted to shake the hand of the little woman who had started a great war (this, incidentally, is the first presidential endorsement in literary history). Despite Honest Abe's help, after an *annus mirabilis*, 1852–53, sales of Stowe's novel slumped. No one quite knows why.

Ten years later, as the bloodiest war in American history raged, both sides – troops in blue and grey – devoured Victor Hugo's *Les Misérables* (1862). So popular was it with soldiers of the Confederate Army that they took to calling themselves, with that self-mocking irony loved by fighting men, 'Lee's Miserables'.

Since it would be thirty years until the US signed up to international copyright, the French author and his estate got not a sou. Jean Valjean's theft of the candlesticks pales by comparison.

What about the modern soldier? In 2006, AbeBooks, an Internet supplier of new and pre-owned reading matter, analysed the top fifty orders received from the war zone in Iraq. Again, it was American soldiery. Rather charmingly, Ouida's romance of the burning sands, *Under Two Flags* (1867), was among the top fifty. It's nice to think of the modern warrior's eyes moistening, under his Ray-Bans, at the thought of Cigarette's heroically throwing herself into the firing squad's fusillade, to save her lover from death.

The top ten novels supplied by Abe were:

The Catcher in the Rye, J.D. Salinger
Harry Potter and the Goblet of Fire, J.K. Rowling
Lonesome Dove, Larry McMurtry
Mostly Harmless, Douglas Adams
The Collector, John Fowles
Devil's Guard, George Robert Elford
The Unwanted, John Saul
The Alchemist, Ken Goddard
Apollyon: The Destroyer is Unleashed, Tim LaHaye
Master of Dragons, Margaret Weis

There is a strong whiff of the high-school curriculum (Salinger, notably) and a lot of fantasy. The presence of LaHaye's vision of Armageddon (and the second coming) happening in the Middle East in the first years of the twenty-first century is slightly troubling. But what is striking is the near-complete absence of male-action war stories. The descendants of Lee's Miserables obviously get enough of that at work.

Well, most of them. There is one example of war-fiction in this top ten: Elford's *Devil's Guard*. It's not a work, nor is Elford an author, with wide name-recognition in what used to be called Civvy Street. But it is evidently cultish among fighting men.

First published in 1971 *Devil's Guard* purports to be the true confessions of a German SS officer, called Hans Josef Wagemueller. The book is generally reckoned to be, and is categorised by merchandisers as, fiction.

The Pesky Definite Article

What do the following famous novels have in common?

The Lord of the Flies
The Heart of Darkness
The Naked Lunch

None of them properly begins with 'The'. Each of them is routinely so miscalled. And, without looking back, is it *The Devil's Guard* or *Devil's Guard*?

Elford's hero recounts his exploits – bloody and genocidal – as a soldier in the Waffen SS, fighting on the Eastern Front, in World War II. The tone is savage and unapologetic. Nazi atrocity is, the narrative asserts (with multiple stomach-churning examples) wholly justified by the inhumanity of the Communist foe.

After the (much lamented) defeat of the Reich, Wagemueller escapes to be recruited into the French Foreign Legion. Under his new flag he fights for France in the Indo-Chinese war against the Communist Viet Minh. More abominable sub-humans, deserving only of extermination. In the Legion with other former Nazis (some 900 of them) he leads the 'battalion of the damned' in daring, and ruthless, guerrilla raids behind enemy lines. Two sequels followed. In the final instalment, Wagemueller has been recruited by the US. His geo-political rampage continues.

Elford is an elusive figure, scarcely more substantial in terms of popular image, than his warrior source, Wagemueller. *Devil's Guard* was, for a long time, an underground bestseller – most reading copies passing from hand to hand. No self-respecting publisher was keen to be associated with what was generally regarded as sickening neo-Nazi pornography. Costs of pre-owned copies are, consequently, sky high. Any British soldier, ordering *Devil's Guard* from amazon.co.uk (in late 2007) would have to pay £35 for the two sole copies in stock.

BOOKS GO TO WAR:
CONTINUED

Penguin, in Britain, had a good Second World War (partly due to the wily ways with the firm's paper allocation of its proprietor, Allen Lane). But, as usual, the Americans did it better; or, at least, bigger. In 1942, the war department's morale branch launched a paperback library designed specifically for the serviceman. The Armed Services Editions, as they were called, were produced on pulp magazine presses, for as little as five cents a copy (they cost GI Joe nothing, of course).

ASE volumes were soft-covered lozenges – twice as long across as down. They slipped easily into a trouser-side pocket or ammunition pouch. The print was large, to reduce eyestrain when read by torch or candle. Some 1,300 ASE editions were produced, comprising 120 million copies. More books were dropped on the American troops than bombs.

What the ASE library provided was, at the top level, Lit 101 and, at the bottom, the cream of the drugstore paperback rack. Everything from Homer, through Mark Twain, to Zane Grey. Virginia Woolf's *The Years* is a prize item for ASE collectors. You'll need a mortgage to buy a copy. The Very Best Seller in the ASE lists was Betty Smith's weepy melodrama, *A Tree Grows in Brooklyn* (1944), which cleared a staggering 95,000 copies. Most GI-Joes, one assumes, longed to be back there with the trees, not 'over there' where the bullets were flying.

I remember the Armed Service Editions fondly. With V-discs (12-inch shellac records, containing the latest swing numbers) and candy ('Got any gum, chum?'), they symbolised the cultural riches of the United States. What I, at least, was fighting for. I read *Moby Dick* (shortened) and *The Great Gatsby* for the first time in ASE editions (my widowed, but vivacious mother was, at the time, dating Americans – lots of candy).

In 2004, it was reported that the Armed Services Editions, in the familiar format, were to be relaunched for the quarter of a million American troops soon to be stationed in the Middle East. It's a tribute to their original designer, Ray L. Trautman, that his 1942 concept still worked.

There was a difference. The new ASEs were relaunched not as a library but as a 'pilot project', organised by freelance philanthropist Andrew Carroll. He described it as 'the biggest giveaway of books in our history, with the possible exception of the Gideon Bibles' (Mr Carroll seemed momentarily to have forgotten the Second World War series).

Carroll's pilot scheme featured a scant four titles: Shakespeare's *Henry V*, Sun Tzu's *The Art of War*, and two current bestsellers: Allen Mikaelian's *Medal of Honor: Profiles of Military Heroes from the Civil War to the Present*, and Carroll's own *Extraordinary Correspondence from American Wars*. 100,000 copies were to be printed as the project's first run.

What did these titles have in common? Stern patriotism. They were books intended to stiffen the sinews of warriors about to biff the evil-doers. Carroll got his sponsorship from an unnamed 'corporate donor' and his selection was approved by the Pentagon.

It flopped.

Seditious Books for the Thinking Soldier

Responding to Carroll's initiative, American sceptics suggested he should add to his list:

Catch 22, by Joseph Heller
All Quiet on the Western Front, by Erich Maria Remarque
Slaughterhouse Five, by Kurt Vonnegut

The Pentagon, one suspects, would not approve.

LISTOMANIA

As the French say, riches embarrass. There are currently more titles published in the UK and US in a month (around 15,000) than even the most bookish person will read in a lifetime. An Elizabethan (with some 2,000 titles then in print, and only a couple of hundred new books every year) could aspire to be, by the standards of the time, well read. We, by the standards of our time, cannot. It's like showering in Niagara. Lists offer a lifeline in the book deluge. We grab at them, like drowning readers.

Decimal-based lists of 'best' books, and bestselling books began to appear in the early twentieth century as book production entered its current out-of-control industrial phase. Biblio-apocalypse.

But listomania is now itself out of control – rampant in the twenty-first-century bookworld: whether it is the bestseller charts (which now contain up to 100 titles, in various categories, weekly), nationwide reading stunts such as The Big Read, or the National Curriculum (currently some 150 works of literature) from which the nation's young are obliged to make their individual lists.

Listomania, like other manias, has its comic aspect. As we saw earlier (p. 96), a 2007 World Book Day poll of 'Books You Can't Live Without' put *Pride and Prejudice* top, five places above the Bible (better luck with the next one, God).

A few months later, David Lassman, mischievous director of the Bath Jane Austen festival, sent out the opening chapters of *P&P* to eighteen leading publishers. Austen's golden prose was barely veiled under the novel's family title, 'First Impressions', as by 'Alison Laydee' (i.e., 'A Lady'), with minimal name changes and the famous 'truth universally acknowledged' opening sentence resoundingly intact.

It resounded not at all. Seventeen of the recipients did not recognise the most essential book in the history of the world. One, Bloomsbury (Harry Potter's publisher), wrote back with the sage consolation that the sample had been read 'with interest' but 'was not suited to our list'. They could clearly live without *Pride and Prejudice*, thank you very much.

Why not, if they've got Harry Potter on the Bloomsbury list?

THE POTTER EFFECT

Literary manias, and concurrent sales bonanzas, are regular events; as regular nowadays as the ocean tides. The only change, it would seem, is that they get even more maniacal with the passing of centuries. Nowadays, they have gone beyond 'curious' into 'totally awesome'.

At the witching hour – midnight – on 20/21 July 2007 the seventh (mystic number) and final instalment of the Harry Potter series (the 'Potteriad') was released. *Harry Potter and the Deathly Hallows* had been kept under the kind of security usually reserved for high-grade plutonium. One guesses that the printers whom the publisher Bloomsbury employed (Clay's of St Ives) were specially selected deaf-mutes, like the servants in nefarious Transylvanian castles where bad things are always happening below stairs.

For up to three days, in the wettest few days on meteorological record, expectant Potter fans camped outside London bookshops. Many were wearing increasingly bedraggled wizard regalia. Their excitement was nothing dampened. The town of Colchester converted its centre into a Hogwarts theme park. Rowling was the biggest thing since Boadicea laid the place waste in AD60.

When the stores opened, at the anti-social hour, it was the literary equivalent of the Oklahoma Gold Rush. And as chaotic. Three million copies were sold in twenty-four hours: a record, outstripping by at least a million the sales of the book's predecessor, *Harry Potter and the Half-Blood Prince*.

Is the Potter Effect a good thing? Insofar as any mania can be approved, some would argue it is indeed a good thing. In a witty letter to *The Times* Books Supplement, 28 July 2007, Edward Kelly wrote:

For those of us who have yet to read any of J.K. Rowling's Potter series there is little to be gained from the current reviews. I did, though, stumble across this statistic that may please some readers: on an average weekend, the emergency room at the John Radcliffe Hospital in Oxford treats sixty-seven children for injuries sustained in accidents. On two weekends, however, only thirty-six children needed treatment: 21 June 2003 and 16 July 2005 – just after the releases of Harry Potter Five and Six. It was suggested at the time that talented writers produce high-quality books for the purpose of injury prevention.

The deduction is obvious: Pottermania is good for children. It keeps them from harm. But does it? The day after Mr Kelly's letter was printed, there were alarmed accounts about a 'damning report' about the 'soaring rate of childhood obesity'. As the *Observer* put it, on its front page (29 July):

> The number of six- to ten-year-olds who become obese will keep rising relentlessly until the late 2040s, with as many as half of all primary school-age boys and one in five girls dangerously over-weight by 2050, according to the document.

For the first time in recent history, Britain would breed a generation of children who could confidently expect to live less long, and less healthily, than their parents.

Those sixty-seven children who, averagely, turn up at the Radcliffe ER would, most of them, have hurt themselves playing. Reading (particularly reading a 600-page book) is the epitome of couch-potatoism. Was the Potter Effect, insidiously, helping rob young fans of their allotted span? Reading is a good thing (hence all those honorary doctorates for services to literacy for J.K. Rowling). But would it not be an even better thing for children to be outside – actively 'doing' something, rather than passively 'reading', or 'watching' something?

JAM, GOLLYS, AND THE S-WORD

It was reported in August 2001 that Robertson's, the maker of fine British jams, were dropping their 'Golly' mascot. Golly, indeed. As the etymologists tell us, that exclamation (beloved by Boris Johnson and Billy Bunter) is a bowdlerisation of the expletive, 'God!', like 'Crikey!' ('Christ's Cross!'). Another Borisism.

Dimly, however, we sense something nastier in the G-word than mild blasphemy. Robertson's adopted its black mascot in the Edwardian period. It was a brilliant marketing stroke. 'Gollywog' brand-marked the product and, in 1928, inspired a spin-off campaign. In return for tokens from the jam pot, kids could get golly brooches and badges to sport on their blazer lapels.

Who invented the 'gollywog'? According to Robertson's commercial mythology, it was them. In their August 2001 press release they asserted: 'Golly was discovered by John Robertson during a business trip to America in 1910. He noticed children playing with a rag doll made from their mother's black skirts and white blouses and thought he could use the idea to sell his product.'

According to the Robertson version, 'gollywog' was an infantile mispronounciation of 'dolly-wolly'. This is wrong. It was actually the brainchild of two English ladies: Bertha Upton and her daughter Florence. The Upton family emigrated to America in 1870 and returned to England (penniless) when Mr Upton died, fifteen years later. In 1895 the Upton ladies enterprisingly wrote a children's book, *The Adventures of Two Dutch Dolls*. Bertha did the text, Florence the illustrations. The hero was 'Golliwogg' [sic] – a lovable (if hideous) 'pickaninny'. Golliwogg was inspired by a minstrel rag-doll which Florence had played with as a child in New York. The book was hugely successful. A dozen sequels had been published by Longmans by 1909 – the year before John Robertson went to America.

Gollys were, in the early 1900s, all the rage in the nurseries of England. Making rag dolls out of discarded mourning garb was easy work in an age when every mother's hand held a sewing needle. Toy manufacturers jumped on the bandwagon.

There was a sideline industry in sewing patterns. Neither the Uptons nor their publisher Longman had secured the copyright, hence it was in the public domain. Florence Upton died in 1922 (aged forty-nine). Her tombstone, in Hampstead cemetery, bears the inscription: 'Creator of the Famous Golliwog'. But not, alas, the owner. Nor, alas, 'famous'.

In short: John Robertson didn't have to go to America. A trip to Hamley's would have done it. Not to mince words, the jam-maker appropriated the Uptons' pretty invention and has never given them credit.

Generations of Britons grew up with gollys in the toybox. And, when the Uptons' books faded from the scene, enter Enid Blyton, in the 1930s, with her series of stories, featuring that lovable trio of tar-babies: Golly, Woggy, and Nigger. No one will regret them fading from the scene.

The other classic racist text of the high imperial age, Helen Bannerman's *Little Black Sambo*, was first published in 1899. It too was a first book by a young woman, inexperienced in the ways of the British book trade. Bannerman's copyright was sold for £5. It went on to make millions for Chatto & Windus.

Little Black Sambo (the more obnoxious a conception, since the lad is Indian, not African) disappeared from bookstores in the late 1990s. Golly(wog) joined him a couple of years later. They were joined in cultural oblivion by a third nostalgic imperial icon. On 10 September 2006, as the *Daily Mail* put it, 'Camp Coffee Is Forced To Change Label By The PC Brigade.'

Since 1885, the bottled coffee essence had displayed a Kiplingesque Scottish officer, in dress-uniform for his camp dinner, being served his post-prandial coffee by a sepoy flunkey. Who says East and West can't meet? The coffee extract was invented at the request of Highland regiments (their officers, that is) who wanted a coffee which could be brewed while putting down native revolts in the Deccan, the jungles of the Punjab, or wherever. Since the mutiny of 1858, India had, of course, been under the direct rule of the Crown. Direct rule was what the Camp label symbolised.

For over a hundred years, the British public bought and consumed the products, without demur and with relish. But in Scotland, in the twenty-first century, Asian shopkeepers, a powerful presence nowadays, from Carlisle to Orkney began to refuse to stock Camp. The Scottish Campaign for Racial Equality was sympathetic. The huge combine, McCormick Foods (a pleasingly Scottish name) yielded, gracefully. On new bottles, the sepoy servant and the kilted officer are depicted both sitting down, sharing a convivial cup on equal terms. Camp comrades. Post-colonialism, one apprehended, was not merely a literary phenomenon.

GO FIGURE

Star Wars (1978) revolutionised the franchise sector of the film industry. What George Lucas created was less a movie than a marketing strategy. The young fan could buy (or persuade parents to buy) *Star Wars* comics, light sabres, and Princess Leia knickers. There were Darth Vader popsicles – a portion of whose sticky revenue dripped back to Star Wars Inc.

The most durable of the spin-offs were so-called 'action figures' – 4-inch dolls for boys and tomboys. They weren't ornaments or cuddle-things. They enabled junior to invent his own battles. The more expensive lines were 'poseable' and had optional wardrobes and arsenals.

The idea originated in 1959, when the Mattel company invented the Barbie doll. Five years later, Hasbro transgendered Barbie with GI Joe – which, to avoid the girly d-word, they called an 'action figure'. A euphemism was born: and with it a profitable industry.

Action figures spun off from kid-oriented movies are now very big business. And American adults, as they grow up, continue to crave their dolls. Given their origins in fables of war and American super-heroism, action figures for (male) adults enjoyed a terrific boost from 9/11. So great was the demand for the George Bush, 'mission accomplished' action figure in 'elite' naval aviator gear that the maker, www.givemetoys.com, had to set up a waiting list. The 'British Ally' action figure – Tony Blair – also sold briskly. For a while. No longer.

There is, happily, a subdivision of the action-figure industry for the book lover. On www.shakespearesden.com (motto: 'Smart Gifts for Intelligent People') there are no less than three Shakespeare literary action figures on offer: a Shakespeare

'Nodder' ('ask him if he likes your poem, and he'll nod approvingly'); a 'L'il William Shakespeare' ('he's a cute little guy!') and 'a Shakespeare poseable action figure' ('this one is all bendy'). All come at a budget-price $8.75 + p&p.

Among other novelties in this webstore, the intelligent person can buy a Poor Yorick Skull for the desk, 'After Shakespeare Mints' to suck, and a Shakespeare 'Celebriduck' ('Rubber Ducks with Soul!') for the bath. While on the subject: if you want Shakespeare condoms they're discreetly procurable at www.dailytidings.com.

12

Wheels

'Certainly not!' replied Toad emphatically. 'On the contrary,
I faithfully promise that the very first motor-car I see,
poop-poop! off I go in it!'
The Wind in the Willows, Kenneth Grahame

WWJD?

In late 2002 there was press and web flurry in America around the conundrum 'What Would Jesus Drive?' It was kicked off by the Rev. Jim Ball, a revivalist preacher, whose Evangelical Environmental Network began running TV ads on that theme in Detroit, home of the American automobile industry.

Ball, the pious owner of a Toyota Prius (a hybrid electric and gasoline vehicle), was exercised about SUVs – gas-guzzlers, with the horsepower of sixteen-wheel trucks, which, due to a quirk in American transport law (a dispensation for 'commercial' vehicles) are effectively subsidised by tax-dollars: as is fuel, consistently half the price that Europeans pay. 'We're helping people understand their choice of vehicle relates to Jesus's message of loving thy neighbour,' Ball said. The guy in the next lane. Given that an estimated 40 per cent of Americans attend church once a week, it was a potent campaign although Motown, where a Toyota Prius is considered the chariot of the anti-Christ, was not the best place to launch it.

Ball's big question was endorsed from a secular quarter by Arianna Huffington, the celebrity columnist. Huffington darkly predicted 'coming SUV wars', as the American public turned against 'these metal monstrosities'. Her ire was specifically directed against the:

Hummer H2, GM's new $50,000 barely domesticated spinoff of the Gulf War darling, which struggles to cover ten miles for every gallon of gas it burns. The symbolism of these impractical machines' military roots is too delicious to ignore. We go to war to protect our supply of cheap oil in vehicles that would be prohibitively expensive to operate without it.

Where did the phrase 'What Would Jesus Drive?' originate? And would Jesus, one might ask, drive, or ride, anything? In the gospel, our Saviour is described as only ever using one form of loco-motion: the ass. He would even walk over water, rather than take a ferry. Would He, two millennia later, have ridden into Jerusalem, like the pontiff, in an armour-plated, plastic-domed Jesusmobile? And what would that converted vehicle be? A Hummer? (never); an SUV? (*surely* not), a Prius Hybrid? (possible), a golf-cart? (be serious – this is the Son of Man). It was a brain teaser for the Christian who wanted to drive God's way on man's highway.

Few who got into the argument, which bubbled toxically on the web, were aware of the literary origins of Jim Ball's WWJD?, as it was acronymised and picked up by the more cynical of the country's car salesmen, who promptly started slapping 'Jesus's Choice!' on the assorted clunkers in their forecourts.

The phrase originates in the Rev. Charles Sheldon's 1896 novel, *In His Steps*. The novel grew out of a series of sermons the pastor delivered in his Congregationalist church in Topeka, Kansas, where – forgotten as he now is elsewhere – Sheldon is still revered as the town's most famous son.

In His Steps was a runaway bestseller and ran for decades. Alice Payne Hackett, in her history of American bestselling fiction, records it as the bestselling ever work of fiction, until block-busters like *Anthony Adverse* and *Gone With The Wind* came along in the 1930s.

The narrative of Sheldon's novel hinges on an opening scene between a clergyman, the Rev. Henry Maxwell (transparently the author), who has an eye-opening encounter with a 'hobo'. Such meetings were all too likely. The years in which *In His Steps* was conceived and published, 1894–1896, were horribly distressed. Following the stock market panic of 1893, there was mass unem-ployment and the worst economic slump ever recorded in North

America. An army of the unemployed was recruited by the populist leader, Jacob Coxey, to march on Washington, D.C. in 1894 under the slogan 'the Commonweal in Christ'. When Coxey's Army reached the capital, on 30 April, it was savagely broken up by the police, and its leaders arrested 'for walking on the White House lawn'.

The crisis was upsetting to men of goodwill, like Sheldon. In his novel, the tramp, before collapsing from starvation at the altar, pointedly asks the clergyman and the congregation '*What would Jesus do?*'

The phrase sticks in Maxwell's mind, and becomes the guiding light for his subsequent good works. The novel went on to inspire a WWJD? movement. Like other revivalist movements it ran its course. But the slogan was revived, on its hundredth anniversary, in the mid-1990s. Devout Christians again started wearing WWJD? lapel buttons and asking awkward questions about personal transportation.

There was no consensus on what our Lord would drive, although general agreement that it probably would not be the civilian version of the Humvee troop-carrier which Arnold Schwarzenegger claimed to have invented, by suggesting the idea to General Motors. Huffington was right about that.

PLATFORM 9¾

A *Guardian* journalist, interviewing John Armitt, CEO of Network Rail, on the development of the King's Cross/St Pancras/Eurotunnel station complex wrapped up with some small talk. It was July 2007 – *Harry Potter and the Deathly Hallows* had just been published. What did the King's Cross people think of it?

Like everyone else, Armitt said, they were fans. But one thing troubled them. Why platform 9¾ for customers travelling to Hogwarts? Platforms 9 to 10 at King's Cross are, like Thameslink, off-station annexes: rather shabby sideshows to the imposing main hall. The description in chapter 6 of *Harry Potter and the Philosopher's Stone*, 'The Journey from Platform 9¾' makes clear that Harry's all-important, but impossible, train leaves from that main hall:

> They reached King's Cross at half past ten. Uncle Vernon dumped Harry's trunk on to a trolley and wheeled it on to the station for him. Harry thought this was strangely kind until Uncle Vernon stopped dead, facing the platforms with a nasty grin on his face.
>
> 'Well, there you are, boy. Platform nine – platform ten. Your platform should be somewhere in the middle, but they don't seem to have built it yet, do they?'
>
> He was quite right, of course. There was a big plastic number nine over one platform and a big plastic number ten over the one next to it, and in the middle, nothing at all.

If one goes to the relevant King's Cross annexe, there *is*, as it so happens, something in between 9 and 10: platform 9b (serving Cambridge, via WAGN, usually). Could this be the explanation?

I think not. If one looks at the back flap of the most recent hardback Potters, one finds the following account of the genesis of the bestselling children's (and latterly 'kidult's') book in the history of the world:

The idea for Harry Potter occurred to J.K. Rowling on the train from Manchester to London, where she says Harry Potter 'just strolled into my head fully formed', and by the time she had arrived at King's Cross, many of the characters had taken shape.

When I travel (uninspiredly, alas) from London to Manchester, or return, I do it from Euston – the station a few hundred yards to the west of King's Cross.

WRONG-HEADEDNESS

There is a stanza in Robert Lowell's 'Skunk Hour', a poem brutally notating the poet's mental crack-up, which often gives British readers problems. It is:

> One dark night
> my Tudor Ford climbed the hill's skull
> I watched for love-cars. Lights turned down,
> they lay together, hull to hull
> where the graveyard shelves on the town . . .
> My mind's not right.

'Hill's skull' is easy, but what is 'Tudor Ford'? Is there some reference here to the Wars of the Roses – are the love cars Plantagenets?

The answer is simple if you're an American of a certain age, a classic car buff, or into hot rods. In the 1930s and 40s, the Ford motor company mass produced a couple of lines of coupé (pronounced 'coop') and sedan. One had two doors, and was called the 'Tudor'. The other had four doors and was called the 'Fordor'. It's a good thing Lowell didn't have one of those. The scansion would have been all wrong.

CELEBRITY CAR CRASH:
NOT A LITERARY THING

Authorship is, by and large, an impoverished and, closeted profession. Behind every glowing word on the page, said George Orwell, you should picture an unshaven hack, in a shabby dressing gown, looking nervously at the clock, a Willy Woodbine drooping, soggily, from his lower lip, as he (for Orwell it was always 'he') coughs his way to the next deadline. Or Proust in his cork-lined room. But never, 'Poop! Poop!', Toad in his toadster-roadster. Famous non-literary people die stylishly on the road. It's their equivalent of the Viking funeral – being pushed out to sea in the community's finest vessel, laden with treasure. When literary people, like Kerouac, are actually on the road, it's most likely someone else is driving.

Everyone knows the car James Dean died in: a Silver Porsche Spyder, one of only ninety available in 1955, nicknamed 'The Little Bastard'. Isadora Duncan died, by strangulation, when her scarf got tangled up in the spinning wheel of her speeding Bugatti. Princess Diana died in a Mercedes S280. Jayne Mansfield – a 1966 Buick Electra. So it goes. J.G. Ballard wrote a novel on the subject of celebrity death cars: *Crash*. I hope the author of that fine work lives for ever. But when he does go to his reward it will not, dollars for doughnuts, be in one of the magnificent vehicles he likes to write about. Literary people take their exits, usually, in other ways.

But a few writers, alas, do die on the road. From the top of your head, in what makes of car did the following authors die? Albert Camus, Roy Campbell, Ross Lockridge, Robert Lowell?

The French author of *L'Étranger* was in a Facel-Vega sports car, with the publisher Michel Gallimard when the automobile (belonging, of course, to the publisher) slid off the road, outside Paris, and ran into a tree, breaking the author's neck. An incomplete manuscript, *The First Man*, was disentangled from the wreckage, to be published thirty-five years later, with some moral trepidation.

Ross Lockridge, the author of *Raintree County* (1955), won what is still the most valuable prize for fiction (in real terms) for the novel. MGM, who were looking for original material they could convert into big-budget films endowed the $150,000 prize (for an account of *Raintree County*, see p. 268). It was Lockridge's first novel. With his sudden wealth, Lockridge bought himself a fine new car, a 'Kaiser'. Limousines of an almost surreal ugliness and gargantuan gas-guzzlingness; the brand was short-lived.

So, alas was the owner. As often happens, Lockridge suffered the authorial equivalent of post-natal depression, together with the crippling sense that he had sold out to the Hollywood philistines. When his baby son urinated on the manuscript of *Raintree County*, Ross ruefully observed he was the best literary critic in the family. That son grew up and eventually published an account of his father's death, by suicide, in the Kaiser, in the family garage:

> His wife found him not in the front seat but in the back. All the car doors were shut. There was no car radio. A vacuum cleaner hose had been hooked up to the exhaust and run through the car's rear ventilation window, which had efficiently been sealed

Star Cars

In a prescient article in the *Boston Globe* on 3 June 1904, the journalist Stephenson Browne predicted that 'the motor car, or the automobile, as one pleases, will probably take the place of the horse in fiction'. Literature has yet to produce a four-wheeled classic of the status of *Black Beauty*, but there have been some notable automobile-centric works of literature. To list them:

1. First enduringly popular work of fiction to introduce the motor car as a major plot element: *The Wind in the Willows* (or 'the poop poop on the road'), 1908. The make of car is unrecorded by Kenneth Grahame.
2. Most luxurious car in literature: the yellow Hispano-Suiza, in Michael Arlen's *The Green Hat*.
3. Cruddiest vehicle in literature: the Joad family's 'Super-Six' Hudson pick-up, in *The Grapes of Wrath*.
4. Most malign car in literature: Stephen King's Christine – a 1958 Plymouth Fury.
5. Most benign car, the 'Paragon Panther' in Ian Fleming's *Chitty Chitty Bang Bang* (1964).

with a large cloth. Her husband's parents and sister arrived before the police, and the sister quickly engineered a family cover up. Aunt Lillian stuffed the death paraphernalia into a garbage can behind the garage, which the police and coroner didn't bother to inspect. Largely acting on the impulse to protect her children from the fact of their father's desertion, my mother agreed with her in-laws to tell police that she had found her husband in the front seat.

The story was given out that he had accidentally banged his head, and fallen unconscious. The garage doors were shut, and the build-up of carbon monoxide had asphyxiated him. The coroner did not go along with it, but the full story remained unknown for forty years.

Robert Lowell died in the back seat of a New York yellow cab, in 1977. He was aged just sixty, and his personal life was chaotic. He was travelling from JFK airport after a disastrous trip to Ireland in which he told his current wife, Lady Caroline Blackwood, that their marriage was finished. The taxi was taking him to the house of his former wife, on West 67th Street, Elizabeth Hardwick. It was a pathetic, but oddly appropriate death, for the poet, whose life had been all twixt-and-tween.

Roy Campbell, immortalised as the poet who assaulted Stephen Spender publicly (at the Ethical Church, in Bayswater) with the screamed (somewhat unethical) accusation 'you fucking lesbian' died in a clapped-out Fiat, in Portugal, where he lived his last years, in 1957. Being a poet, and hard up, he had neglected to get a fatally bald tyre fixed.

Campbell is the author of the second-best-ever poem about motorcycles, 'Dreaming Spires' – in which the gauntleted-begoggled bard screams across the South African veldt, halting only to wonder at a herd of giraffes.

> Respiring fumes of pure phlogiston
> On hardware broncos, half machine
> With arteries pulsing to the piston
> And hearts inducting gasoline:

Buckjumping over ruts and boulders,
The Centaurs of an age of steel
Engrafted all save head and shoulders
Into the horsepower of the wheel –

The best ever two-wheeled poem is Thom Gunn's 'On the Move'. On the two-wheel good, four-wheel bad theme, there are relatively few works of well-known fiction about bicycles. The best, for my money, is H.G. Wells's *The Wheels of Chance* (1896).

13
Morbid Curiosity

'If my doctor told me I had only six minutes to live,
I wouldn't brood. I'd type a little faster.'
Isaac Asimov, who died, aged ninety-two, leaving behind
him over 500 books, in nine out of the ten categories of the
Dewey Decimal Library Classification System.

WHAT KILLED ANTHONY TROLLOPE?

On 12 July 2007 the 'great literature' component of the National Curriculum excluded Thackeray from the list of set authors. It perversely (to my partisan mind) included the 'lesser Thackeray' (as G.K. Chesterton labelled him): Anthony Trollope.

Trollope would not have resented Chesterton's valuation. It is true that, thanks to TV adaptation, the Chronicler of Barsetshire has a larger profile nowadays. But placing himself above the author of *Esmond* would have infuriated Trollope. In his autobiography, he cites Thackeray (his friend and literary idol) as the greatest novelist ever to have written.

Trollope was, as contemporaries testify, rather easily infuriated. Legend has it that irascibility killed him – or, at least, precipitated his death. It began in Garlant's Hotel in Suffolk Street. Outside, Trollope heard the sound of a German brass band – a popular form of street entertainment in the late Victorian period. Trollope, for obscure reasons, loathed them. He equally loathed barrel organs. Why, no one knows. For him they were what the scream of a 747 overhead is to the residents of Heathrow: intolerable. They maddened him.

He rushed across the room, threw open the window, and shouted furiously. It was injudicious for a man with terminal *angina pectoris*. A few days later, the country mourned his death. Death by tuba and hurdy-gurdy. The death certificate, of course, read differently.

What killed *Mrs Stalin?*

Stalin's wife, Nadezhda Alliluyeva, shot herself dead in 1932. The details only became public in the late 1980s. Her motive for suicide, however, remains obscure. One explanation was her appalled reactions to the forced agricultural collectivisation and consequent mass starvation of the Russian peasantry. By her bed was discovered a copy of Michael Arlen's romantic novel, *The Green Hat*. The novel pivots on a suicide, which a character commits because he believes he has syphilis. This was a sophisticated theme for the time. The novel was made into a film, in 1928, starring Greta Garbo which – because of the impropriety of Arlen's narrative – was retitled *A Woman of Affairs*. It is an odd last novel for Mrs Stalin to have been reading. More so, perhaps, in light of the persistent suspicion that Stalin was infected with syphilis.

DYING WELL: TOO WELL

One of the urban myths of literature is that Douglas Adams, creator of the arch-whimsical *The Hitchhiker's Guide to the Galaxy*, departed this life furiously pedalling to nowhere on his exercise bicycle in his beach-house at Malibu. Too Arthur Dent for words. And too good not to pass on – chortlingly.

Having encountered this misrepresentation of what actually happened on innumerable occasions, and in print, M.J. Simpson, Adams's biographer, was moved to write a weary letter of correction to the *Guardian* (14 June 2003) – a paper which (like myself, alas, elsewhere) had gleefully propagated the vulgar error:

> Your article ('Is it possible to be too fit?' June 10) perpetuates the myth that the author Douglas Adams died while riding an exercise bicycle. Although Adams' heart attack did strike him during an exercise session at his local gym, he was not actually exercising at the time. In the documentary film *Life, the Universe and Douglas Adams*, his close friend Chris Ogle describes how Adams passed away while lying down on a bench, ready to do some sit-ups. Adams did frequently use an exercise bicycle, but that was not what robbed us of his talent. It may be a minor point, but I feel it is best to nip such misinformation in the bud.

Alas, such buds are not easily nipped. Many famous last literary words, for example, are too good to be true; and too good not to circulate for ever because of that. Goethe's last words, *'mehr licht, mehr licht'* (more light, more light), are almost certainly apocryphal. Certainly apocryphal is Oscar Wilde's everywhere circulated: 'either that wallpaper goes or I do' (the wallpaper it was that stayed – but see p. 240).

Anton Chekhov's wonderfully aimless last words are, however, multiply vouched for as entirely genuine: 'I am dying. I haven't drunk champagne for a long time.' Nor would he, for even longer, unfortunately.

A Star to the End

When Barbara Cartland passed away in 2000, a few weeks shy of her ninety-ninth birthday, she was planted in her back garden in Camfield Place beneath her favourite tree: an ageless English oak. Perry Como's version of 'I Believe' was played as her coffin was lowered. The coffin was made of cardboard.

THE WALLPAPER ACTUALLY DID GO

On 30 November 2000, exactly one hundred years to the day after Wilde's death, the news channel CNN reported:

> The shabby flowered wallpaper in the hotel room where Oscar Wilde died on 30 November, 1900 has been replaced by vibrant blue-green frescos as part of a refurbishment of the former Hotel d'Alsace pension house on the Left Bank. The first-floor room, a mix of greens, reds and gold, has been redecorated in the style of Wilde's London apartment and the walls are based on designs by Wilde's contemporary Aubrey Beardsley, who illustrated some of his work.

For the record, and deflatingly, according to Richard Ellmann's authoritative biography, Wilde's quip was, in point of fact: 'My wallpaper and I are fighting a duel to the death. One or the other of us has to go.' It was uttered a full month before his death.

But who wants to know that? The *mot* always came first with Oscar. Or last, in this case.

THE WERTHER EFFECT

One could make a strong case for Goethe's *The Sorrows of Young Werther* (1774) as the first modern bestseller in that it did not merely sell like hot cakes, it also triggered a sales mania – and another interesting mania as well.

Epistolary in form, the narrative centres on the hopeless love of the young hero for the unattainable Charlotte ('Lotte'). Unattainable, because she is promised to another, Albert, in marriage. Werther yearns, beautifully, and impotently, for what he will never have. Elopement and adultery are out of the question. And Albert, although a decade older than Lotte, looks good for decades to come.

So overpowering is Werther's love that he resolves on what the Germans call '*liebestod*'. He duly shoots himself (with a pair of pistols supplied by Lotte's fair hand) on the stroke of midnight, with the final ejaculation: 'Charlotte, Charlotte! farewell, farewell!'

They are also the last words of Frankenstein's doomed monster, before he hurls himself off into the frozen polar wastes and certain death. The lab-born creature has, we were earlier told, taught himself to read, Dick-and-Jane fashion, from *The Sorrows of Young Werther*. Mary Shelley was clearly an enthusiast. She was not alone. The whole of Europe in the early nineteenth century was 'puking in Wertherism', a wholly unenthusiastic Carlyle complained.

Literary epidemiologists will note that Goethe's book is the first identifiable mania in fiction. It drove people crazy, as the fabled bite of a tarantula spider is said to make its victims dance uncontrollably (the 'tarantella') before expiring. Young men, volume in hand, donned Werther's idiosyncratic canary-yellow trousers, open-necked shirt (a style picked up by Byron, another fan) and sky-blue coat. I have sometimes wondered whether the blue coat which Mr Bingley is described as wearing on his first visit to Longbourn, in *Pride and Prejudice*, indicates that Austen, like Mary Shelley, was a clandestine Wertherist. Goethe's was not, one fancies, a book which would have looked appropriate on the coffee table at Chawton.

Imitation went fatally far beyond trousers. There were, it is said, some 2,000 suicides by young male admirers of the novel. Goethe himself commented, wonderingly, on the holocaust his work had innocently and unintentionally provoked. Readers, he noted:

> thought that they must transform poetry into reality, imitate a novel like this in real life and, in any case, shoot themselves; and what occurred at first among a few took place later among the general public.

Authorities went so far as to ban Goethe's book, on grounds of public safety. The ripples extended far beyond eighteenth-century Germany. On his deathbed in the Washington Hospital, brought there prematurely, aged thirty-nine, by drink, Edgar Allan Poe was heard to say: 'the best thing a friend could do for me is blow out my brains with a pistol'. He wanted a beautiful, Wertherian quietus, not a drunkard's squalid death and burial in Potter's Field.

The imitative garb, and the melodramatic suicide technique, were examples of what social-psychologists call 'memeticism', or 'copy-cat' behaviour. Novels, films, plays have, occasionally, the power to do this. And, sometimes, as with *Werther*, it leads to suppression. Stanley Kubrick's 1971 film adaptation of Anthony Burgess's *The Clockwork Orange* allegedly triggered youth violence of the kind perpetrated by Alex and his droogs (whose sartorial excesses go far beyond canary-yellow trousers). The director suppressed any showing of the film in the UK for many years.

So clear-cut an example of the memetic tendency was Goethe's novel that in 1974, the University of California sociologist, David Phillips, coined the term 'The Werther Effect' to describe it. In his field work, Phillips had been researching whether suicide, if dramatic and widely publicised, was 'contagious'. Could you, bluntly, catch suicide, like the flu? Yes, Phillips discovered, you could. And he called the phenomenon after Goethe's hero.

THE BASKERVILLE EFFECT

Professor David Phillips, the sociologist who coined the term 'Werther Effect' (see above) is clearly more bookish than many of his number-crunching kind.

In the December 2001 issue of the *British Medical Journal* Phillips outlined his current research into the 'Baskerville Effect'. 'I have often wondered if people could indeed die by fright,' he explained:

> and if so, how this could be investigated quantitatively. I recalled that in *The Hound of the Baskervilles*, Sir Charles Baskerville dies of a fatal heart attack, apparently because he is frightened to death by the hound. Since Arthur Conan Doyle was a physician as well as an author, I wondered if his story was based on medical intuition or literary license, i.e., were fatal heart attacks and stress linked in fact as well as fiction?

As with his Werther research, Phillips's investigative method was elegant and rigorously empirical.

In Mandarin, Cantonese, and Japanese, the words 'death' and 'four' are pronounced nearly identically, and consequently the number 'four' evokes discomfort and apprehension in many Chinese and Japanese people. Because of this, the number 'four' is avoided and omitted in some Chinese and Japanese floor and room numberings, restaurants, and telephone numbers. In addition, the mainland Chinese air force avoids the number 'four' in designating its military aircraft, apparently because of the superstitious association between 'four' and 'death'.

Using the computerised death certificates of 20,000 Asian-Americans in San Diego, Phillips discovered that death rates did indeed peak on the fourth of the month. Death-day, that is. Specifically, there was consistently 13 per cent more mortality among the selected population on that day from cardiac arrest than the average rates would predict. Theory proved.

It is, however, a nice question as to whether a suddenly glimpsed numeral on the kitchen calendar could have the same, blood-chilling, effect that Dr Watson describes:

A hound it was, an enormous coal-black hound, but not such a hound as mortal eyes have ever seen. Fire burst from its open mouth, its eyes glowed with a smouldering glare, its muzzle and hackles and dewlap were outlined in flickering flame. Never in the delirious dream of a disordered brain could anything more savage, more appalling, more hellish be conceived than that dark form and savage face which broke upon us out of the wall of fog.

Alas, as he confesses, piffling 'ethical' issues prevented Professor Phillips from loosing a pack of hounds from hell on the Asian-American citizenry of San Diego.

CAUSE OF DEATH:
GEORGE ORWELL

A minor confirmation, albeit unscientific, of Professor Phillips's thesis is supplied by the newspaper fuss provoked by the broadcast of the TV adaptation of Orwell's *Nineteen Eighty-Four*, on Sunday 12 December 1954.

The 'Horror Show', according to the *Daily Express* front page, caused death by shock to Beryl Merfin, as she sat – transfixed by the horrors of Room 101 – on her sofa in Herne Bay. Questions were asked in the House. The BBC responded, to their credit, by repeating the programme four days later. They added an 'unsuitability' warning for those 'with weak nerves'. Nerves were weaker at the time (as I can testify myself, having shuddered joyously through the programme: now *Saw IV* provokes barely a bored yawn).

There was some sex, as well – mildly, but hardly lethally, shocking; even in 1954.

MORE WERTHERISMS

Suicide, one may say, is the sincerest form of literary flattery. Those thousands of young men who blew their brains out clearly read *The Sorrows of Young Werther*. But, in their memetic frenzy, did they read the text carefully enough?

One asks, because the founder of the Hemlock Society for

Assisted Death, Derek Humphry, argues strongly against the gun to the temple as a favoured 'final exit'. Notoriously, if aimed from that point, the round, is quite likely not to kill – or, at least, not instantly – leaving the victim to languish for hours (or, like the luckless James Brady, who took a bullet in the temple for Ronald Reagan, in 1981, languish for the rest of a long and horribly disabled lifetime).

In 1875, one of the sons of the man of letters, Thornton Hunt, chose to shoot himself in the London Library: the genteel place, set up in the city's clubland as an alternative to the British Museum Reading Room (a place rendered unendurable for gentlemen scholars, Carlyle complained, by the 'man with the bassoon nose').

Thornton Hunt had enjoyed an 'open union' with G.H. Lewes's wife; Lewes at the time was in an 'open union' with George Eliot (who says the Victorians were Victorian?) There was a complicated web of parentage.

Hunt's son chose to kill himself during the library's opening hours, in the journals room. He was reading, the librarian later recorded, G.H. Lewes's *Problems of Life and Mind*. He evidently did not find any solution to his own problems there. He took out a Derringer pocket pistol, and shot himself in the head.

Library staff heard the report and wondered what it was. Gunfire was rarely heard in the stacks. Then, three minutes later, they heard a second shot. They rushed to see what it was. Evidently what happened is that Hunt aimed the firearm at his temple and the bullet ricocheted to an area of the skull where it did no fatal harm. A second agonising shot was required to finish the grisly business. Not quite, though. The staff found the young man 'blood and brains oozing from his head, but still alive'. He died, on his way to hospital, two hours later.

Thomas Carlyle, happened to be in the building at the time.

His only comment on being told what had happened was: 'another of Thornton Hunt's bastards gone'. He was infuriated that the fuss meant he could not get a book he urgently needed and he demanded a member of staff fetch it for him. The man had to step across the body of the dying Hunt to do so.

GRAHAM GREENE: WERTHERIAN

Inefficient as it manifestly is, the dramatic pose of the gun to the temple, or the side of the head, is irresistible. It looks, somehow, 'right'. Knowing the risks (not of suicide, but messily failed suicide) this rather undermines the effect of Graham Greene's account of his early experiments with Russian roulette. He, too, was clearly a latter-day Wertherian.

As he recalls, Greene was afflicted in early 1923, not by hope-less love, but by paralysing ennui. Desperate remedies were called for. He found a revolver ('a small ladylike object') belonging to his brother Raymond, in a desk drawer. He loaded the weapon with one bullet, and strolled into the deserted woods by Berkhamsted Common. He then span the chamber, put the muzzle 'into my right ear' and pulled the trigger.

The drastic medicine worked. His ennui lifted. Addicted to the gamble, Greene tried it on five subsequent occasions over the next few months. As he recalls:

> It was ... during the Christmas of 1923 that I paid a permanent farewell to the drug. As I inserted my fifth dose, which corresponded in my mind to the odds against death, it occurred to me that I was not even excited: I was beginning to pull the trigger as casually as

I might take an aspirin tablet. I decided to give the revolver – since it was six-chambered – a sixth and last chance. I twirled the chambers around and put the muzzle to my ear for a second time, then heard the familiar empty click as the chambers shifted.

Had the spinning chamber landed on the live round, Greene might well have been unlucky enough to have survived decades as a vegetable. Unglamorous, and not what he had in mind at all.

As Derek Humphry and other connoisseurs of easy ways to die (alas, Cleopatra's asp is entirely fictional) explain: if you *must* do it with a hand gun (and please don't – some poor sod has to clean up later) you should put the barrel in your mouth, and aim up through the soft palate, avoiding the tough barrier of the skull (see The Hemingway Solution, p. 141). But this is wholly undramatic and inelegant. One does not look dignified on the way to eternity with six inches of gunmetal stuck down one's gob.

Actually, the inefficiency of the gun-to-the-temple technique was clearly spelled out by Goethe himself, who evidently researched the question. As the finale of *The Sorrows* recounts, a single shot was heard by a neighbour at midnight. Thereafter, deathly silence:

In the morning, at six o'clock, the servant went into Werther's room with a candle. He found his master stretched upon the floor, weltering in his blood, and the pistols at his side. He called, he took him in his arms, but received no answer. Life was not yet quite extinct.

The surgeon who is called in determines that 'the bullet, entering the forehead, over the right eye, had penetrated the skull'. A temple shot that is. It had not killed him. It is not until noon, twelve agonising hours later, that 'Werther breathed his last.' It allows, of course, a poignant *omnium gatherum* around his deathbed, but Werther's is a hideously botched suicide.

On the other hand, if Werther had had access to Mr Humphry's manual, and used the approved method, how could he – with a pistol between his teeth – have ejaculated his final 'Charlotte! Charlotte! Farewell! Farewell!'?

Fiction, as ever, prefers the beautiful over the practical.

DYING WELL?
OR DEAD DRUNK?

On his deathbed, literary legend has it, Joseph Addison summoned his dissolute stepson to witness how 'a Christian can die'. (The cause of death, interestingly, was asthma – see p.27). Addison had, his biographer records: 'studied attentively the deaths of Augustus, Socrates, Petronius Arbiter, Seneca, Cato and Sir Thomas More'. In various essays he had defined the ideal exit as a dignified combination of classical stoicism and Christian humility and like the 'winding up of a well-written play'.

How beautiful is death, when earn'd by virtue!

Addison has the hero declare, in his well-written play, *Cato*.

Alexander Pope professed to find Addison's ostentatiously vaunted 'virtue', and his life- (and death-) long habit of gathering acolytes around him to admire that Addisonian quality stomach-turning (nor did he much like that pompous *Cato* play). He duly satirised the other writer as 'Atticus', in the 'Epistle to Dr Arbuthnot', and as a prig on a self-erected throne, who would:

> Like Cato, give his little senate laws,
> And sit attentive to his own applause.

It was typical that Addison would want applause as he breathed his last, expiring to the sound of sycophantic, but decently muted, clapping, from his faithful claque.

The anecdote about deathbeds and dissolute stepsons is wholly Addisonian (or Atticus-like, if one is feeling catty) but, alas, possibly 'of dubious authority', as beautiful literary anecdotes often are. According to the sardonic Horace Walpole: 'unluckily Addison died of brandy – nothing makes a Christian die in peace like being maudlin.'

HART CRANE: DEATH BY WATER (AND WHISKEY)

A similar (beautiful or boozy?) enigma hangs over the death of the American poet Hart Crane. It was 1932 and Crane was thirty-three: Jesus's age – the period of that 'shadow line' in life, as Conrad calls it. Psychoanalysis sees this age as a critical threshold in artists' lives. Pass the mid-life crisis, and an author qualifies for a 'late phase'. Many do not. A surprising number of great writers die in their thirties or early forties, never passing the shadow line. What, one wonders, might Scott Fitzgerald, Dylan Thomas, or the Brontë sisters not have given us, had they lived as long as, say, W.B. Yeats?

Hart Crane would never cross his shadow line. He had already, in 1932, established his claim to greatness with his New York poem, 'The Bridge' – a magnificent ode to the mighty link between the Brooklyn and Manhattan boroughs. 'Our myth' he called the majestic bridge. At the time of his death (the Conrad reference is appropriate) he was on board ship – travelling from Central to North America.

Crane's was a massively troubled talent. While on a Guggenheim Fellowship in Mexico in 1931–32, his chronic drinking had spun out of control, triggering troughs and peaks of alcoholic depression and drunkard's elation. As an artist, and in his personal life, Crane was fascinated by the places between – bilaterality – and the heroic human acts (such as the Brooklyn bridge, or oceangoing ships) which could throw spans across, or connect, separated places.

Bisexuality, however, was something Crane could never quite bridge – or, at least, not so as to be comfortable in being two things sexually at once. Normally homosexual in his preference, he was, at the time of his suicide, on the rebound from a heterosexual affair with Betty Cowley, the wife of his patron, the critic Malcolm Cowley. She was on board Crane's death-ship.

All the pieces were in place when, on 27 April 1932, Crane removed his topcoat (romanticised accounts add that he lit a cigarette) and 'vaulted', wearing only pyjamas, over the stern-rail of the *Orizaba*. Eight bells had sounded: it was midday: the transitional moment of the circadian cycle. He was *nel mezzo del camin di sua vita*. The vessel was 250 miles north of Havana, and ten miles east off the coast of Florida. In the middle of the seas. The artistic composition of the act was perfect. And final. 'Man overboard!' was called ('Poet Lost!' would have been more appropriate – and more poetic). After two, fruitless, hours searching the voyage resumed: Craneless. The sharks had got him, the captain thought. The Gulf of Mexico was a bridge the poet would never cross.

Was the act conceived as a kind of 'life-poem' – something which posterity can unequivocally admire? Was Crane, to paraphrase Addison, showing the world how a poet can die? As nobly, that is, as Empedocles throwing himself into Etna?

There is, as with Addison, a less beautiful explanation. So chronically drunken was Crane on the trip that Peggy Cowley had him locked by the steward in his cabin at sundown. But in the night before, Crane had broken out and made for the crew's quarters. There he had made sexual advances to various sailors – some accounts say a 'cabin boy'. He may have had sex with more than one of the crew. It was not joyful. He was savagely beaten up and robbed of his wallet and his personal jewellery. The steward found him in his room on the morning of his suicide his face still bloody, his eyes blackened, well into the first bottle of whiskey of the day. His last authenticated words were 'I'm utterly disgraced.' He may have feared prosecution when the ship reached port.

In this version of the event, Crane killed himself not as a beautiful act of artistic self-definition but because he felt really bad. Posterity can decide which version it prefers: the poetic, or the squalid. Myself, I go for the poetic. Although if he really *had* to do it, I would have preferred Crane to have waited and jumped from the Brooklyn bridge.

DYING CONSCIENTIOUSLY

There is no ambiguity about what qualifies as the most conscientious death recorded in the annals of literary history. In August 1889, on his deathbed, Wilkie Collins found himself only a third of the way through the novel he was currently serialising in the *Illustrated London News*, *Blind Love*. The undertaker would, he realised, beat him to the *finis* line. Collins did not, as had his friend Dickens, intend to leave any authorial threads dangling.

Incompletions

Great works of literature, left uncompleted by the untimely visit of the Grim Reaper:

The Mystery of Edwin Drood, Charles Dickens
Don Juan, Lord Byron
Denis Duval, William Makepeace Thackeray
Answered Prayers, Truman Capote
The Autobiography of Benjamin Franklin
The Landleaguers, Anthony Trollope
Wives and Daughters, Elizabeth Gaskell
The Last Tycoon, F. Scott Fitzgerald
Sanditon, Jane Austen
Islands in the Stream, Ernest Hemingway

Death, one concludes, is a lousy literary critic.

He therefore commissioned his friend, Walter Besant, to complete the novel for him: which the other novelist loyally did. 'Tell him I would do the same for him if he were in my place,' Collins said, in a note accompanying the instruction, together with a full scenario as to how the narrative of *Blind Love* was to work out.

The novel, as completed by Besant, was not a success on the *Woman in White* scale (although a modern PR agency could have put a fair wind in its sails with the dramatic circumstances of its composition). But the plot revolves around an interesting, and oddly appropriate, idea: a faked photograph, ostensibly taken of a corpse, which is used for insurance fraud. Wilkie's mind, ingenious to the end, invented a deathbed gimmick as he lay on his own deathbed. Conscientious, yes. And brilliant.

WHAT WAS THAT HE SAID?

Dylan Thomas was given to the flamboyant gesture, particularly when confronted by female beauty and even, legend has it, *in articulo mortis*. Alcohol also was of lifelong interest to him. All witnesses agree, it shortened his life (as did, to harp on the subject, asthma).

Legends have accreted, limpet-like, round Dylan's drinking. They should be taken sceptically. Drinkers invariably lie about quantity (downwards to the policeman with the breathalyser, upwards to their drinking mates). As the biographer Paul Ferris records, Thomas claimed in his youth to have drunk forty pints of beer at a sitting (with many trips to see men about dogs, one imagines). 'An unlikely feat', Ferris adds; perhaps unnecessarily.

For years after the poet's premature death at thirty-nine, the legend circulated that following an epic debauch through the bars of Manhattan, Thomas returned to the Chelsea Hotel, on West 23rd Street, to throw himself on his knees before a leggy beauty – later identified as Elizabeth Reitell. She was organising the off-Broadway production of *Under Milk Wood* and currently warming his hotel bed. IDMT ('it doesn't matter on tour', as theatrical people say).

In this devotional posture Thomas, as one folkloric variant of the legend has it, announced: 'I've had eighteen straight whiskies, I think that's a record. I love you.' Like the proverbial Highlander, the wild Welsh boy liked two things in life naked: whiskey and women. Whether it was a personal record or one which he fancied might have had a chance with the *Guinness Book of Records* is unclear.

The story of Dylan's last bout, with subsequent heroic embell-
ishments, originates with John Malcolm Brinnin's indiscreet
memoir, *Dylan Thomas in America*. Brinnin is regarded as a Judas
by card-carrying Thomas admirers. The remark about the record-
breaking binge, allegedly, was Thomas's last coherent utterance
on earth, before going gentle into the good night.

An equally dramatic account, is given by the artist Jack Heliker,
who helped Reitell with the paralytic Thomas in his hotel room,
just prior to his being shipped off to hospital. According to Heliker,
Dylan Thomas's last words were: 'After thirty-nine years, this is
all I've done.' Eighteen whiskies, thirty-nine years: take your pick.

Thomas collapsed and was taken off to St Vincent's Hospital, coma-
tose. Six days later he was dead of what the doctors labelled 'acute
insult to the brain' – and, one might add, a terminal compliment to
female beauty and the potency of Old Grandad Kentucky bourbon.

It is not only drinkers who lie about their intake. History does
as well. On the proprietary site www.lochlomonddistillery.com,
for example, Thomas's intake is expanded by the makers of Loch
Lomond's fine tipple to 'nineteen straight whiskies'. The declar-
ation nestles alongside Humphrey Bogart's similarly famous last
words, 'I should never have switched from Scotch to Martinis.'

But even this enlarged number pales beside veritable tsunami
of liquor reported by *New York Post* 'gossip dowager' Cindy Adams.
In 2006, she told readers of her column that a film by John Maybury,
was in prospect. Entitled *The Best Time of Our Lives*, it would:

> star Lindsay Lohan and Keira Knightley. It's about Wales's most
> famous poet, Dylan Thomas, and his wife who'd earlier been in
> show business, Caitlin MacNamara. Dylan Thomas's entire life was
> a drunken haze. Years ago I visited Greenwich Village's White
> Horse Tavern where, after downing seventy-nine straight whisky
> shots, he died in '53.

Stony Farewells

Probably the longest literary-lapidary farewell is that found on the tombstone of John Keats, at the Protestant Cemetery, Rome

THIS GRAVE
CONTAINS ALL THAT WAS MORTAL
OF A
YOUNG ENGLISH POET
WHO
ON HIS DEATH BED
IN THE BITTERNESS OF HIS HEART
AT THE MALICIOUS POWER OF HIS ENEMIES
DESIRED
THESE WORDS TO BE ENGRAVED ON HIS TOMB STONE
'HERE LIES ONE WHOSE NAME WAS WRIT IN WATER.'
JOHN KEATS

Among the shortest must be Emily Dickinson's (composed by herself in typically terse style), on her plaque, at Amherst, Massachusetts:

CALLED BACK

It's the precision of 'seventy-nine' which sticks in the mind. Assuming that a shot in the White Horse is, as is usual in the US, twice the British pub measure, this pans out at something over two bottles. Straight. Without question an acute insult to brain and body.

Enter the 'authoritative' biographers, with their adherence to boring fact. They have established that Thomas probably had no more than half-a-dozen shots of Old Grandad that fatal night. It was, more likely, the drugs (Cortisone, ACTH, morphia) that the incompetent doctors pumped into him that carried him off.

'GOOD CAREER MOVE, TRUMAN'

Like other too-good-not-to-repeat insults, Gore Vidal's spiteful witticism on hearing of the death of Truman Capote in 1984 has been much recycled.

It is as true in literature, as anywhere else, that as the 1930s song put it, 'Nobody loves you till you're dead and gone.' Some highly successful literary careers have not got off the ground until their authors were long under it. Gerard Manley Hopkins among canonical poets, was a total unknown to the poetry-reading public until thirty years after his death. His literary resurrection was entirely thanks to his friendship with the poet laureate, Robert Bridges – a figure over whom, ironically, time has thrown much heavier spadefuls of forgetful earth than ever covered his obscure Jesuit friend. For every million schoolchildren who read 'The Windhover' not one, nowadays, would even know the name of Bridges's magnum opus, *The Testament of Beauty*.

The most curious example of authorial rising from the grave is John Kennedy Toole, who committed suicide in 1969 aged thirty-two, wholly unknown as an author. Unknown, unpublished, but not unloved. The eminent Southern novelist, Walker Percy, was, at the time, working as a writer in residence at Loyola University New Orleans. As Percy recalls:

> While I was teaching at Loyola in 1976 I began to get telephone calls from a lady unknown from me. What she proposed was preposterous ... her son, who was dead, had written an entire novel during the early sixties, a big novel, and she wanted me to read it. Why would I want to do that? I asked her. Because it is a great novel, she said ... if ever there was something I didn't want to do, this was surely it: to deal with the mother of a dead novelist ... I read on. And on. First with the sinking feeling that it was not bad enough to quit, then with a prickle of interest, then a growing excitement, and finally an incredulity: surely it was not possible that it was *so* good.

The narrative – unsurprisingly perhaps – centred on a gloopy young man's relationship with his domineering mother, in steamy New Orleans.

A Confederacy of Dunces was duly published, won a posthumous Pulitzer Prize, became an instant bestseller and a work of cult fiction to rival *The Catcher in the Rye*. The hyper-intellectual comedian, Stephen Fry, resolved to adapt it for film – but the same curse which prevented Toole's masterpiece getting into print seems to operate with getting it on to celluloid. A pity, since the combination of this pair of quizzical minds would work.

Toole's title alludes to a witticism of Jonathan Swift's: 'When a true genius appears in the world, you may know him by this sign, *that the dunces are all in confederacy against him.*' He evidently anticipated rejection of his genius by the dunce-world. And one wonders whether, like D.H. Lawrence's murderee (who puts himself out to be killed) he actually courted rejection, as a kind of bitter confirmation of his worth, and the impercipience of the herd.

Would Toole have defied the dunces, as belatedly he did, had the author not put black wings on the scruffy manuscript of *A Confederate of Dunces* with his suicide? If Stephen Fry immolated himself, ritually, on a pyre of *QI* scripts, in frustration with his abortive Toole project, would the film materialise, handsomely financed, from the embers?

The wittiest fantasia on the 'best of career moves' is Max Beerbohm's short story, 'Enoch Soames'. A doomed 1890s poet (doomed less by genius and debauchery than utter mediocrity), steeped in absinthe and feeble decadence, Enoch sells his soul to the devil. He does so in return for a passport which will enable him to visit the Round Reading Room of the British Museum, one hundred years after his death, to relish what he is confident will be posthumous fame.

Not much has changed in the library, AD 1997, Enoch discovers. It's a bit like H.G. Wells's far future in *The Time Machine*: egg-hairless people, all wearing woollen 'sanitary' uniforms and as indistinguishable from each other as battery chicks.

Enoch's time-trip turns out disastrously. After a desperate scour of the catalogues, the only reference to himself he can discover is on page 234 of '*Inglish Littracher 1890–1900* bi T.K. Nupton, publishd bi th Stait, 1992', where he reads that:

a riter ov th time, naimed Max Beerbohm, hoo woz stil alive in th twentith senchri, rote a stauri in wich e pautraid an immajnari karrakter kauld 'Enoch Soames' – a thurd-rait poit hoo beleevz imself a grate jeneus an maix a bargin with th Devvl in auder ter no wot posterriti thinx ov im! It iz a sumwot labud sattire, but not without vallu az showing hou seriusli the yung men ov th aiteen-ninetiz took themselvz.

Enoch Soames, that is, survives as a fictional character in 'Enoch Soames'. Trapped in the text: Jacques Derrida could not invent it.

Enoch Soames Day, 3 June 1997, was celebrated in the magnificent Round Reading Room – where Karl Marx, George Bernard Shaw, and innumerable Soamesian literary forgettables had worked, but neglected to make any deal with the Prince of Darkness for their return. Soames himself was eagerly looked for, but did not appear. He would, as the story predicts, have recognised the magnificently unchanged structure: the brainpan of the nation, as Thackeray called it.

A year later, that structure ceased to exist when, in June 1998, the new St Pancras site opened and the old 'RRR' was converted into a tourist canteen and souvenir boutique area. Some cynics alleged (and most Soamesians would like to think) that the removal was deliberately delayed – so that the luckless Enoch would not land in a building site. There was enough disappointment awaiting the 'thurd-rait poit' without that.

The Reading Room desks and seats were subsequently disposed of to the antique salvage firm, Lassco. I forlornly made some enquiry as to Karl Marx's seat and desk, but they had no record of it.

Curious Connections: a Terminal Quiz

'Curiosity is one of the permanent and certain
characteristics of a vigorous mind.'

Samuel Johnson

QUESTIONS

1. What is the connection between Carter's Little Liver Pills and George Moore's novel, *Esther Waters*?

2. What is the connection between the film *Reservoir Dogs* and a bestselling novel by Edward George Earle Bulwer-Lytton?

3. What 'pallor' connects Clint Eastwood and the mass poisoner Graham Young?

4. What vowel separates the poet Robert Browning's only published obscenity and a children's book by Roald Dahl?

5. Which is the only major railway station in Britain to be named after a novel?

6. What do the following novels have in common (apart from the fact you haven't read them)?: *His Family, The Secret City, Raintree County, Something to Answer For*? What, partneringly, do *My Antonia, Night and Day, The Naked and the Dead, The French Lieutenant's Woman* have in common (apart from the fact you've read them)?

7. Who is the odd man out: Winston Churchill, Saddam Hussein, Iain Duncan Smith, Jeffrey Archer?

8. Ditto: D.H. Lawrence, Clive Barker, Ian McEwan.

9. What do the following works of literature have in common and which is the odd one out: the Anglo-Saxon epic, *Beowulf*,

Stephen King's *Carrie*, James Joyce's *Stephen Hero*, Carlyle's *The French Revolution*?

10. Which two bestselling novels in 2007 had the same title – and what connection, if any, was there between the respective subject matters?

ANSWERS

1. *What is the connection between Carter's Little Liver Pills and George Moore's novel,* Esther Waters?

The novelist Pearl Craigie (1867–1906), the most accomplished Catholic novelist of the nineteenth century, was born into an American family, enriched by their patent medicine, Carter's Little Liver Pills (motto: 'Wake up your liver bile!'). The family moved to London where Pearl was brought up. She published her first story aged nine. Like George Eliot, she chose to write under a masculine pseudonym, 'John Oliver Hobbes'. After a disastrous marriage, in which her cad husband infected her with venereal disease (no pills for that, alas, in 1890), she took up with the novelist, George Moore, best known to posterity as the author of *Esther Waters*, the story of a sexually abused woman.

A more principled novelist than he was a human being, Moore too, proved caddish, and the couple spent many years writing revenge novels about each other, to the huge amusement of those in their circle in the know.

A believer in education for women (but not votes for them)

Craigie/Hobbes endowed a prize for essay writing in the English department, at UCL – the first department in the country to admit women undergraduates (only allowed on campus with chaperone until the twentieth century; see Theodora Bosanquet, p.149). Winners of the 'Hobbes' routinely assume their award is named after the author of *Leviathan*.

No one reads John Oliver Hobbes any more nor, apart from *Esther Waters*, George Moore. Nor does anyone cure themselves with the patent medicine which made Craigie's life so materially comfortable. The US Federal Trade Commission, in April 1951, determined that the pill's relationship to the liver was remote (the active ingredient, bisacodyl, is principally a laxative). Under protest the product was renamed 'Carter's Little Pills', languished on the shelf, and died.

2. *What is the connection between the film* Reservoir Dogs *and a best-selling novel by Edward George Earle Bulwer-Lytton?*

In 1828, Bulwer-Lytton published a 'fashionable novel', *Pelham: Or the Adventures of a Gentleman*, which took London by storm. In it, the dandy hero decrees that a gentleman should only wear dark, funereally dark, suits. Exit the colourful finery of the Regency.

As Carlyle sarcastically observed in his 'Body Dandiacal' digression in *Sartor Resartus* (a satire on the extravagances of fashion), *Pelham*'s injunction was taken as holy writ. It still rules today. The dark suit is, of course, the hallmark of the criminal gang in Quentin Tarantino's 1992 film

3. *What 'pallor' connects Clint Eastwood and the mass poisoner Graham Young?*

Clint Eastwood plays the murderous 'Preacher' in the 1985 Western (directed by Eastwood) *Pale Rider*. The mass poisoner Graham Young (memorialised in the 1995 film, *The Young Poisoner's Handbook*) was, it is often suggested, inspired to use his toxin of choice, the 'undetectable' and lethal thallium, by Agatha Christie's 1961 novel, *The Pale Horse*. Christie was famously good on poisons. Young was dubbed 'the teacup murderer' by the tabloid press – the friendly 'cuppa' being his preferred way of administering thallium to his luckless victims. Clint kills his victims more straight forwardly, with the most powerful handgun in the world.

4. *What vowel separates the poet Robert Browning's only published obscenity and a children's book by Roald Dahl?*

In his poem *Pippa Passes* Robert Browning used the word 'twat' under the misapprehension that it referred to an item of nun's attire:

> Then owls and bats
> Cowls and twats
> Monks and nuns in a cloister's moods
> Adjourn to the oak-stump pantry.

The poet, intending no naughtiness, had been misled by a sarcasm about an ambitious churchman in the seventeenth-century poem, 'Vanity of Vanities':

> They talk'd of his having a Cardinal's Hat
> They'd send him as soon an Old Nun's Twat.

Roald Dahl published his superselling book for children, *The Twits* (illustrated by Quentin Blake), in 1980.

5. *Which is the only major railway station in Britain to be named after a novel?*

Waverley Station, in Edinburgh, is named after the title of Scott's 1814 novel. The name is particularly appropriate, since the GNER station is a main terminus for the London/Edinburgh, English/Scottish connection. Edward Waverley fights ('wavers') under both flags in the novel, and can justly be called an Anglo-Scot.

6. *What do the following novels have in common (apart from the fact you haven't read them)?:* His Family, The Secret City, Raintree County, Something to Answer For? *What, partneringly, do* My Antonia, Night and Day, The Naked and the Dead, The French Lieutenant's Woman *have in common (other than the fact that you have read them)?*

A curious curse of utter oblivion lies on the first novels chosen by judges for newly launched, high-prestige, literary prizes. Every one a clunker.

The first such prize for fiction in the US, the Pulitzer, chose as its inaugural laureate in 1918 Ernest Poole, on the strength (so to call it) of his novel, *His Family*. The story of a New York patriarch, Poole's work has been deeply out of print for decades. The judges of a prize indelibly associated with the New York newspaper world may have been biased by the fact that the central character, Roger Gale, runs a news-clipping agency. Nothing like leather, as cobblers used to say. The judges should, of course, have chosen Willa Cather's *My Antonia*. Perhaps none of the metropolitan Pulitzer panel had a soft spot for that author's rural Nebraska.

The James Tait Black prize (judged by the Regius Professor at Edinburgh) came up in 1919 with a title scarcely better known to today's public than Mr Black (an Edinburgh publisher) himself, Hugh Walpole's *The Secret City*. Even among Walpole's not very memorable *oeuvre* (his most enduring work is *Rogue Herries*) this is an obscure effort. A more enlightened Regius professor would have chosen Virginia Woolf's *Night and Day*.

Again, one can see why *The Secret City* might have been chosen. Its hero is a young war-wounded officer turned diplomat who is sent to Russia in December 1916 – the eve of Revolution. In John Reed's vivid phrase, Henry Bohun sees the future, and, by God, it might just work. There was huge curiosity and nervous optimism about the great Soviet experiment in 1919. Walpole's (sadly inaccurate) hope was 'that the two souls, Russian and English, so different, so similar, so friendly, so hostile, may meet'. Historically right for the mood of the period of its publication subsequent history reveals the novel as sentimental and intellectually foolish. Not that that intellectual foolishness ever stopped a novel winning a prize.

Raintree County, Ross Lockridge Jr's attempt to outsplash *Gone with the Wind* was the winner of the 1948 MGM Prize. The cash value of the prize, $150,000, is still the largest ever offered the novel. Lockridge's American Civil War epic (1,066 pages in its first published version, the original manuscript, before cutting, weighed in at twenty pounds) was as big a flop as the bundle of Louis B. Mayer loot thrown at it. Equally a flop was the 1957 Montgomery Clift–Elizabeth Taylor starring MGM blockbuster movie spun off from the novel.

'The most expensive movie ever made' (as the PR people called it), *Raintree County* hastened the end of the old studio system, as America turned to the small screen in the living room.

It was gloom all round. Lockridge never recovered from the humiliation, spiralled into depression, and committed suicide two months after the publication of *Raintree County* – his first and last novel. He killed himself with the exhaust fumes of the new car, in the garage of the new house, which he had bought with his vast money prize (see p. 231). At least he did not survive to see the movie.

Making the film shattered (permanently) the health of Clift (who almost died in a catastrophic car crash during filming – which drastically altered his facial appearance) and Taylor (obliged to wear crippling corsets to bring her somewhere near the wasp-waistedness of Vivien Leigh as Scarlett O'Hara).

Had they been looking for a 1948 novel worthy of their prize, the MGM judges should, of course, have chosen Norman Mailer's *The Naked and the Dead*.

P.H. Newby's *Something to Answer For* was the first winner of the Booker Prize for fiction, in 1969. Why the first panel should have chosen this work has always been something of a mystery. Its current standing, in the annals of literature, is summed up by the two forlorn tags attached to it in the current Amazon catalogue: 'no customer reviews yet [after thirty-eight years!]. Be the first.' And 'Availability: Currently unavailable. We don't know when or if this item will be back in stock.' The choice for 1969, which posterity would approve, would probably be John Fowles's *The French Lieutenant's Woman*.

The choice of Newby's, decent but sexually unadventurous, novel is perhaps explained by the presence of Rebecca West on the Booker panel. During one of their deliberations she was heard to say, 'If I read the sentence "he entered her" once more I shall buy a doormat with "welcome" written on it for English fiction.' Lots of entering in *The French Lieutenant's Woman*.

7. *Who is the odd man out: Winston Churchill, Saddam Hussein, Iain Duncan Smith, Jeffrey Archer?*

They have all published novels (Hussein no less than two while undergoing trial). They were all, with the exception of Archer, leaders of political parties. Archer was merely Deputy Chairman of the Conservative Party. He too wrote while in prison, but memoirs not fiction. Some would say.

8. *Ditto: D.H. Lawrence, Clive Barker, Ian McEwan?*

Lawrence and Barker are exhibited artists, as well as distinguished novelists. McEwan does not paint – at least for public admiration. None the less at a Downing Street party, the newly elected Tony Blair in 1997 congratulated the author, saying how much he liked his work, and that he had actually bought two McEwan paintings.

9. *What do the following works of literature have in common and which is the odd one out: the Anglo-Saxon epic,* Beowulf, *Stephen King's* Carrie, *James Joyce's* Stephen Hero, *Carlyle's* The French Revolution?

Near or actual destruction is what these four works have in common. Stephen King wrote *Carrie*, his first published novel, while working all day as a schoolteacher, living in a trailer park, with two young children howling in the background. In despair he threw the manuscript in the trash can. It was retrieved by his loving wife, Tabitha, published in 1973, setting him up for his subsequent phenomenally successful career.

James Joyce, in a similar fit of rage and despair at a depressed period in his early career, threw the manuscript of *Stephen Hero* in the fire. It, too, was saved from the flames by his wife, Nora.

Carlyle entrusted the manuscript of the first volume of his magnum opus, *The French Revolution* (his only copy), to John Stuart Mill to read. Mill's maidservant, coming on the manuscript near the fireplace in front of which her master had been reading it the night before, used it to light the house fires (see p. 58). Unluckily, the faithful Jane Carlyle was not around, like Tabitha and Nora, to rescue her husband's brain child.

That we have the 3,000-line Anglo-Saxon epic *Beowulf* is thanks to some anonymous monk who transcribed the then centuries' old poem in the tenth century. This manuscript passed through various hands until it was acquired in the seventeenth century by Sir Robert Cotton. Let the British Library, current custodian of the manuscript, take up the narrative at this point:

> Cotton was a keen collector of old manuscripts whose library was presented to the nation by his grandson in 1700. However, the dilapidated state of Cotton's house gave cause for concern over the collection's safety. The library was moved first to Essex House in the Strand, then to Ashburnham House in Westminster. In 1753, the Cotton collection found a home in the newly founded British Museum ... On 23 October, 1731, Ashburnham House was ravaged by a fire that destroyed or damaged a quarter of Cotton's library. *Beowulf* was saved with other priceless manuscripts, but not before its edges were badly scorched.

An unknown hand threw the ms out of the window.

10. *Which two bestselling novels in 2007 had the same title – and what connection, if any, was there between the respective subject matters?*

The novels in question are *Kingdom Come*(s). In June 2007, the paperback edition of J.G. Ballard novel by that name* was selected by Waterstone's as one of their three-for-two promotional items, ensuring handsomely enhanced sales.

* The hardback edition was first published in September 2006.

Ballard's novel is typically apocalyptic (using the term loosely). Richard Pearson, returns (in his Jensen Interceptor) to Brooklands after his estranged father's murder, by random spree shooting, in the Metro Centre – a huge, ultra-modern shopping mall, like 'a spaceship that's just landed', or a Millennium Dome crossed with one of Dante's circles of hell. The murder, and what follows, is – as usual with Ballard – ominous in the extreme.

Meanwhile, riding high on the *New York Times* bestseller list (on which it enjoyed number-one position when it was released in May 2007) was *Kingdom Come* by the latter-day prophet Tim LaHaye, and his faithful scribe, Jerry B. Jenkins. Subtitled *The Final Victory*, it's the sixteenth and last instalment of the 'Left Behind' saga.

Begun in 1995, it is, its publishers, Tyndale House, claim, 'the fastest-selling adult-fiction series ever' ('adult-fiction', I can't help thinking, is not quite the right epithet). The series has sold 43 million copies to date.

The LaHaye–Jenkins *Kingdom Come* is, unlike Ballard's effort, literally apocalyptic. A fictionalisation of the Book of Revelation, LaHaye's 'end-times' narrative began with the 'rapture' of the righteous into heaven. There followed seven years of 'Tribulation' in which the left-behind not-quite-so-righteous did valiant battle with Anti-Christ and his 'New Order' (thinly disguised Kofi Annan and the UN) culminating in Armageddon, the conversion of the Jewish 'remnant' (most, alas, go down to the fiery pit, along with two billion Muslims), the establishment of God's Rule in Israel (no 1967 boundaries here) and – at last – the Second Coming.

The series was designed to synchronise with the millennium, and got a huge boost from 9/11 – a moment at which the 'rapture index' (i.e., the signs of imminent apocalypse) went ballistic (see www.raptureready.com).

Left Behind evangelicalism helped Bush in both his successful election campaigns. This last volume is profoundly uneasy.

LaHaye's final scenario is hilariously lacking in finality. Jesus has returned to earth. The date of his 'glorious appearing' is fuzzy, but clearly now(ish): 2007. The Saviour has brought with him an entourage of angels, Old Testament worthies (including Noah), saints, and the recently raptured. 'Everyone is assigned temporary housing until Jesus reconstructs the earth.'

Reconstruction, though, will take a thousand years. Miraculously, everyone now speaks Hebrew 'fluently'. The novel is written in American baby-talk, interspersed with undigested King Jamesisms. Those who have already made it to heaven are ageless. They're also sexless – which one can't help thinking takes some of the fun out of salvation.

The fighters for Christ during the Tribulation live for a thousand years. But, like Swift's Struldbrugs, they age and get pretty motheaten. They witness the second final judgement from wheelchairs, c. 3007. The Christ-deniers (they're still around) live to a paltry hundred, before the fiery pit swallows them up. Lucifer himself appears to lead his massed Christ deniers in yet another 'final' battle. Armageddon II. No contest. Jesus lifts his finger and 'Satan's entire throng – men, women, weapons, everything – was vaporised in an instant.' The Pentagon should be so lucky.

Why are so many Americans reading *Kingdom Come*? God only knows. And God help any Left Behind fan who picks up Ballard's *Kingdom Come* by mistake. There is, it is probably unnecessary to note, no copyright in titles – unless trademarked. Ballard (who got there first) probably wishes there was.

Index

'To enter the palace of Learning at the great gate, requires an expense of time and forms; therefore men of much haste and little ceremony are content to get in by the back door.'

Jonathan Swift (despiser of indexes)

Some Indical Curiosities

Best indical jest: William F. Buckley, in the complimentary copy of his latest book, inscribed by the index entry 'Norman Mailer':

> Hi! Norm! Knew you'd look here first!

Best novel with an indexer hero: Philip Hensher, *The Fit* (it is not, alas, an extensive field of literary endeavour).

When did Indexing start? Not, as is commonly thought, with the invention of printing in the 15th century, but with the rise of the universities, two centuries earlier.

When will Indexing end? With the googleization of all knowledge, at some point in the second decade of this century (some say).

Wittiest Indexer: according to H.B. Wheatley (1838–1917), the father of modern indexing, the palm goes to James Russell Lowell; such as in this example from the *Bigelow Papers* (1861):

> No, a monosyllable. Hard to utter.

The vote among the current Society of Indexers goes to Francis Wheen, for his index to *How Mumbo-Jumbo Conquered the World* (2004). For example:

> *Blair, Tony*, claims descent from Abraham, 165; defends secondary picketing, 216; defends teaching of creationism, 7, 113–15; displays coat-hangers, 224; emotional guy, 205, 207, 210, 212; explores

Third Way, 226; likes chocolate-cake recipe, 51; sneers at market forces, 217; takes mud-bath in Mexico, 130–1; venerates Princess Diana, 201–2; worships management gurus, 57.

Wisest thing ever said about indexing: H.B. Wheatley (again):

Bad indexers are everywhere and what is most singular is that each one makes the same sort of blunders.

INDEX

THE END OF THE BOOK

The codex book (i.e. what you are holding) is the most vener-able piece of cultural technology we have. In its printed form, it's been around for half a millennium. And the codex manu-script can be traced as far back as ancient Rome. Perhaps further.

It's astonishingly unchanged over these centuries. Gutenberg could have made something very like what's in your hand, as could his stylus-wielding predecessor, Gutenbergus. The codex book seems to have emerged perfectly-formed at birth. And in-destructibly the same thing – even amidst all the technological scurry of the last century. A book is a book is a book: whether Caxton made it, or Random House. Innumerable death sentences have been served on the codex. None has yet come to pass.

But, perhaps,at long last, the end is nigh. In the same month that this book is published, Waterstone's will, it is announced, start selling Sony ebooks along with their Gutenbergian wares. Exit ink, paper and codicality. And, after the ebook? Who knows? Neural transfers of information, via pseudo-telepathic comm-unication? Huxley foresaw something of the kind in *Brave New World*'s hypnopaedia, where learning is poured via the ear into the child's sleeping brain. In the Keanu Reeves 1995 film version of William Gibson's cyberpunk fantasy, *Johnny Mnemonic* (a regular contender in 'all-time turkey' competitions) the hero has 160 giga-bytes downloaded into his bonse in much the same way as I will back this current file onto my hard disk. And so fast is IT advancing that sf, even Gibson's, has difficulty keeping up with it (Johnny Mnemonic still uses 3.5 floppies – as futuro-anachronistic as Keanu's wearing spats and plus-fours).

Suppose reading does give way to new, more Gibsonian, modes of information transmission – would it matter? Arguably, it would: at least according Maryanne Wolf, in her 2008 book, *Proust and the Squid: the Story and Science of the Reading Brain.*

Professor Wolf is expertly qualified, as Director of the Center for Reading and Language Research at Tufts University. She argues that reading inked words on a white page is not merely an acquired skill – like five-finger typing or tap-dancing. It physically and irreversibly remoulds the infant brain. Put another way, our primal reading experience re-routes our wiring. For the rest of our lives. Reading makes us the human beings we are. Or, as Wolf puts it:

> Computer scientists use the term 'open architecture' to describe a system that is versatile enough to change – or rearrange – to accommodate the varying demands on it. Within the constraints of our genetic legacy, our brain presents a beautiful example of open architecture . . . Thus the reading brain is part of highly successful two-way dynamics. Reading can be learned only because of the brain's plastic design, and when reading takes place, *that individual brain is forever changed, both physiologically and intellectually.* [My italics]

Ah yes, Professor Wolf, But what if that all-important reading does not 'take place'? The bookless world of the future will create children with radically different cortical structures. A new species will emerge from the cyberslime and the digitosoup. Call it the Postscript, or PS generation. The supralits. Think, perhaps, of the children in *Village of the Damned.* But nicer (one hopes).

Us book-readers, with our primitively-wired book brains, will be like the Neanderthals in the face of the new-age homo sapiens as they rise from their electronic cradles. And where are the Neanderthals now?

A grimly curious thought to end a book on.